Against the Current

Teresa Pritchard

Against the Current

Teresa Pritchard

This book or parts thereof may not be reproduced in any form, stored in a retrieval system, or transmitted in any form by any means—electronic, mechanical, photocopy, recording, or otherwise—without prior written permission of the publisher, except as provided by United States of America copyright law.

Copyright ©2021 by Teresa Pritchard

All rights reserved

ISBN Paperback: 978-0-578-97444-6

Printed in the United States of America

To Lilly, Abby, Kanen, Amelia, and Banks. Oh, how I want you to understand God's love for you! The desire of my heart is for you to live from the place of being fully known and fully loved by God. You bring my life so much joy and I hope you know you are my favorites!

To my husband, Wesley. Thank you for sacrificing time to allow me to birth what God puts in my heart for others. I love you.

To my family who allows me to dream and works beside me to bring it to pass. I am blessed by your talents and stand in awe of how God gifts me with each of you.

To my Fayetteville Community Church family. You exemplify LGLEO (Loving God- Loving Each Other). I am honored to serve the kingdom alongside you.

To the women and girls who hold this book in your hands. I have been praying for you. I pray you know how much God loves you. You are chosen. You are called. You are His.

To my Lord and Savior Jesus Christ ... my lifeguard and anchor. I dedicate my all to you!

Table of Contents

Chapter One: Chosen 1

Chapter Two: Called 17

Chapter Three: God is with You 21

Chapter Four: The Current 27

Chapter Five: God's Plan 33

Chapter Six: Set Apart 39

Chapter Seven: Lifeguards 43

Chapter Eight: Anchors 61

Chapter Nine: Keep Swimming 85

About the Author 102

Chapter One: Chosen

What does "being popular" mean to you?

I believe most people have a desire to be popular, even if it is a secret desire. I think it would be an interesting experiment to ask your friends to define popular. I bet you will find as many different opinions as the people you interview. While you may find varying opinions of what popularity is, I'm pretty sure you will also find a common denominator. People are looking for self-worth, approval, and a place to belong. They are just looking for it in all the wrong places.

There is a high price for popularity because it is based on the admiration and approval of people. The problem with that is the price for their approval keeps changing because one thing I know for sure… people are fickle. I realize "fickle" is not a word you may use very much but I like it! It rhymes with pickle, and I find it funny that "fickle" and "pickle" totally relate to what I am trying to relay here. People can be sweet one day and sour the next…just like pickles. Hey, that's it! People are fickle pickles! What they want today is no longer satisfying tomorrow and they quickly move on to something or someone else. I get dizzy trying to keep up. Okay, okay, I know that was a little bit corny but stick with me anyway. We can all use a little laugh once in a while, right?

We **all** are looking for approval and acceptance. We all want to feel like we belong. We all want to know that we matter, that we are seen, recognized, and loved. But we will never find it in people. They don't have it to give us because they too are looking for the same thing. Doesn't that explain why we post on social media and spend the next few hours checking and rechecking the number of "likes" and comments we receive? We are looking for approval. We want people to like our post, but our *real* desire is to know people like *us*. There seems to be a false sense of value and importance if the "likes" numbers are high. Why do we give so much power to the "fickle pickle people" to determine our worth? That can be dangerous. It can confuse us about who we really are and cause us to lose ourselves trying to measure up. In our search for popularity, we give too much power to other people we hardly know to decide for us what we like and who we like as we try to live up to so many different expectations. Have you ever felt like you woke up one day realizing you drifted so far from where you wanted to be, and you don't even know how you got there? Maybe it was because you tried to live up to expectation after expectation from person after person wanting so much to fit in that you lost your way.

Is that where you are right now? Maybe that is why God made sure you picked up this book at this very moment. Beautiful Girl...I want you to know that God sees you. He knows everything about you, and He is wild about you! You already have a place to belong. You already have God's approval.

Psalm 139 was written so you would know God's love and thoughts toward you.

Lord, you know everything there is to know about me. You perceive every movement of my heart and soul, and you understand my every thought before it even enters my mind. You are so intimately aware of me, Lord. You read my heart like an open book, and you know all the words I'm about to speak before I even start a sentence! You know every step I will take before my journey even begins. You've gone into my future to prepare the way, and in kindness you follow behind me to spare me from the harm of my past. You have laid your hand upon me!

Every single moment you are thinking of me! How precious and wonderful to consider that you cherish me constantly in your every thought! O God, your desires toward me are more than the grains of sand on every shore! When I awake each morning, you're still with me. Psalm 139:1-5, 17-18 The Passion Translation

God has laid his hand upon you because **he chose you**. He chose you because he loves you. All his thoughts toward you are good. You can never escape his love for you.

Yes, you are chosen. Do you understand what that means? God did not play the game, "eenie,meeny, miney, moe" to choose you. NO! God was very intentional when He chose you. You have been chosen according to the foreknowledge of God. (1 Peter 1:2) That means

God's choice is not random. God chose you before you ever knew anything about Him!

Jesus said, "The world would love you as one of its own if you belonged to it, but you are no longer part of the world. I CHOSE YOU to come out of the world, so it hates you." John 15:19 NLT

"I have told you all these things so that you will not fall away from your faith." John 16:1.

Jesus wants us to know the world has a pull and flow. Everything about the world runs opposite from God. The world values pleasure, wealth, ambition, and sensuality. Think of the world like a powerful river flowing with a very strong current. We are all born into it. We have no choice in the matter just like we have no choice in our DNA or who our parents are. But let's take a closer look at John 15:19 and fill in the blanks.

"The world would love you as one of its own if you belonged to it, BUT you are _____ part of the world. I _____ you to come out of the world……." John 15:19

God, because of his great love, chose **you**. He wants to set you apart from the flow of the world because he sees something very special about you. But He gives fair warning…. the world hates anything and everything that resembles Him. He warns about this so you won't fall away from faith and will have strength to stand against the world's current.

Here are two more Scriptures that affirm you are chosen.

Circle the word **chosen** in each verse and underline anything else that assures you just how much God adores you.

Deuteronomy 14:2

"For you are a holy people to the LORD your God, and the LORD has chosen you to be a people for Himself, a special treasure above all the peoples who are on the face of the earth" NKJV

1 Thessalonians 1:4 NIV

"For we know, brothers and sisters loved by God, that He has chosen you"

Did you see it?

You are chosen.

You are God's treasure.

You are loved.

Yes, we are all born into this world, this river of life, and that is how our stories begin. But there is a day in your life that God calls your name because He chose YOU! He wants to be your Heavenly Father, your provider, your rescuer, and friend. Your response to His call is your choice but it is God's desire for all people to answer with a resounding, "Yes Lord!" We can see this in 1 Timothy 2:4, "(*God*) who wants all people to be saved and to come to a knowledge of the truth." NIV (italics is my own addition for emphasis)

This verse of Scripture clearly lets us know that God chooses us for salvation. He wants to save us from the sweeping current of this world. He offers us a choice to be saved, yet not all people are saved. Remember, it is our choice. God did not create us as robots. He wanted to give us a free will to decide for ourselves if we would choose to love Him in return. God also wants us to come into the knowledge of the truth. That means God wants us to understand the truth and this includes the idea of understanding what is right about Him. He wants us to know that He is good. He wants us to know above all things He wants to bless us. He wants us to know His desire is never to harm us and most importantly He wants us to know His unfailing love for us.

If we can grasp the truth of God and His love for us, we would realize there is nothing that can ever separate us from His love.

Romans 8:38-39 (NLT) assures us of this.

And I am convinced that nothing can ever separate us from God's love. Neither death nor life, neither angels nor demons, neither our fears for today nor our worries about tomorrow-not even the powers of hell can separate us from God's love. No power in the sky above or in the earth below—indeed, nothing in all creation will ever be able to separate us from the love of God that is revealed in Christ Jesus our Lord.

Beautiful Girl…Oh how I want you to understand God's love for you! The desire of my heart is for you to live from the place of being fully known and fully loved by God. His perfect love for you will cast out all fear of not being enough, not measuring up, not being seen, and not fitting in.

God is always speaking. His voice is a gentle whisper saying, "I love you." He is constantly reassuring you of His love. But there is another voice competing for your attention. It is the voice of the enemy, and it is everything but gentle. It is the voice of fear.

You get to choose which voice you listen to.

FEAR NOT

God's voice will always bring you to His peace. The enemy's voice will bring confusion, fear, and chaos.

When I hear the voice of fear and feel the cares of life overtaking me like a flood, I pick up my Bible and turn to Isaiah 43:1-3. Scripture is God's love letter to us.

"Fear not, for I have redeemed you…. I have called you by name; you are mine. When you pass through the waters, I will be with you; and through the rivers, they shall not overwhelm you…. For I am the Lord your God……" Isaiah 43:1-3 (English Standard Version)

I love this passage of Scripture for many reasons. First of all, God begins with two words that I think we need many times in our lives: FEAR NOT. He knows we are human and that this world can be scary! Did you know there are over 365 references in Scripture telling us not to fear? That is at least one for every day of the year! Sometimes we may be afraid of something simply because we don't understand it; or maybe we don't know the truth about it. Remember in the previous paragraph I told you God wants us to understand the truth about Him? God knows when we understand the truth about His goodness, His kindness, His faithfulness, and His love toward us, we would never fear Him. God knows it is not fear that drives us to Him, but rather His unexpected and generous kindness that opens up a pathway for us to be drawn to Him. These few verses in Isaiah 43 gives us many reasons not to fear God or anything else in this life. This is just too good not to dive in for a closer look.

Fear not. Remember this is God speaking. How do you hear His voice? Do you hear him saying, "Fear not" with sternness like a drill sergeant getting in your face with a command? Do you hear Him speaking to you with disappointment or anger? I hope you hear Him saying "Fear not" with love and compassion as He wraps His arms around you to assure you there is nothing to be afraid of because of His presence.

I have redeemed you. When you hear the word, "redeem" or "redemption" in church or read it in the Bible, it is always referring to Jesus and what He did for us on the cross. To help get a better grasp on its significance I looked up the word "redeem" in the dictionary. There were four main definitions: to buy, to pay off, to get back, and to exchange.

In ancient times, redeem was often referred to buying a slave in order to free them.

Who did Jesus buy? Us! The Bible tells us we are not our own, but we have been bought with a price. (1 Corinthians 6:19-20) Jesus paid the price that sin demanded. Death. He redeemed us to set us free.

What did Jesus pay off? He paid off the debt we owed for our sin. It was a debt we could never pay because according to the Bible, the price for sin is death. That means we would have to die for our sins. Jesus died on the cross to pay for every sin we would ever commit. His shed blood paid our debt in full so we could live. "For the wages of sin is death, but the gift of God is eternal life through Jesus our Lord." Romans 6:23

What did Jesus get back? Us! We needed a way to get back to God. What separated us from God? Sin did!

TIME OUT. I want you to imagine I just hit the pause button on the TV remote right in the middle of a movie to give you a little bit of background, so the rest of the movie makes sense. Let's answer the question, why do we need redeeming in the first place?

The Bible tells us in the book of Genesis that in the very beginning of time God created the earth and all that is within the earth so He could make a suitable place for man to live. Then He created the first man and woman and named them Adam and Eve because God wanted a family of His own. The Bible tells us God is love (1 John 4:16) and love needs something to give itself to. God created the Garden of Eden with every plant and fruit tree imaginable so Adam and Eve would not only have a beautiful place to live but would have food to enjoy. God walked and talked with Adam and Eve every day. He loved them and He enjoyed hanging out with them. He put them in charge of the earth and told them they had access to everything in the garden with the exception of one particular fruit tree. God set that one tree aside for Himself but gave everything else to Adam and his wife, Eve to enjoy. God told Adam not to eat the fruit of that forbidden tree because it would open his eyes to evil and would cause him to die. I'm sure you probably know what happened next. Satan came along in the form of a slippery snake, and he began a conversation with Adam's wife, Eve. Can I stop right here to give you a little warning? NEVER give the devil the time of day! He will always come to you to tempt you to doubt God and His Word. Anytime there is even the slightest hint of doubting God, walk away. Or better yet, go get your Bible and thump the devil over the head with it! Let's get back to Eve. When

Satan appeared on the scene with Eve, the first four words that slithered out of his mouth have caused people problems ever since!

"Did God *really* say…?"

Satan will always come to discredit God's Word and try to make us question it.

Let's see what God actually said to Adam.

Genesis 2:15-17 (NIV)

The Lord God took the man and put him in the Garden of Eden to work it and take care of it. And the Lord God commanded the man, "You are free to eat from any tree in the garden; but you must not eat from the tree of the knowledge of good and evil, for when you eat from it you will certainly die."

Now let's return to the conversation the serpent had with Eve in Genesis 3:1 (NIV)

"Now the serpent was craftier than any of the wild animals the Lord God had made. He said to the woman, "Did God really say, 'You must not eat from any tree in the garden'?"

Compare what God actually told Adam to what Satan asked Eve.

Genesis 2:15-17 NIV	**Genesis 3:1**
The Lord God took the man and put him in the Garden of Eden to work it and take care of it. And the Lord God commanded the man, "You are free to eat from any tree in the garden; but you must no teat from the tree of the knowledge of good and evil, for when you eat from it you will certainly die."	"Did God really say, 'You must not eat from any tree in the garden'?"

First of all, have you ever seen a talking snake? Me either. Satan is a spiritual being and the only way he can interact with human beings is to embody a living thing. That is another book for another day. I just wanted you to know Satan entered into the snake using it and abusing it to get to Eve. She would not have known to fear the snake. There was no fear at this point. Fear came *after* Adam and Eve sinned.

Now compare the two conversations in our texts. Can you see how Satan distorted God's instruction? God told Adam he could eat from *any* tree in the garden except one. Notice how Satan turned the words around, "Did God really say, 'You must not eat from *any* tree in the garden'?" Do you see the difference it makes in the slightest twist of words? Satan made it look like God was withholding all the trees of the garden when in reality God told them they could eat and enjoy every tree except one.

Satan still uses the same tricks on us today. He will take the Word of God and twist it around trying his best to make us stumble. That is why it is important for us to take time to read the Bible for ourselves asking God to help us understand what He wants us to know and help us live by its instructions. We must be careful not to take God's Word out of context or misquote it to make it say what it does not say. A lot of people stumble over this making poor decisions and mistakes that bring painful consequences. God gave His Word to us to teach us, to correct us, and to instruct us in goodness. (2 Timothy 3:16) His ways will never lead you wrong. The only thing God is hold back from you is pain! He is not trying to keep you from having a good time. It has always been God's desire from the very beginning to give His kids the very best. He wants us to know Him, to love Him, and to enjoy our lives. God wants to provide everything you need for life and happiness. He has given us His Word so we can know Him and His character. His Word will guide you and protect you if you will obey it. Just remember, He is always going to give His Word for your **good**.

Let's continue the conversation between the serpent and Eve. Genesis 3:2-4 (NIV)

The woman said to the serpent, "We may eat fruit from the trees in the garden, but God did say, "You must not eat fruit from the tree that is in the middle of the garden, and you must not touch it, or you will die." "You will not surely die," the serpent said to the woman. "For God knows that when you eat of it your eyes will be opened, and you will be like God knowing good and evil."

Two things I want you to see here. First: Eve added to God's original instructions to Adam. Eve told Satan, "We may eat fruit from the trees in the garden, but God did say 'You must not eat fruit from the tree that is in the middle of the garden, <u>and you must not touch it</u>, or you will die.'"

God did not say anything about not touching the forbidden tree. As a matter of fact, Genesis 2:15 clearly tells us God took Adam and put him in the garden to work it and take care of it. There was only one thing Adam could *not* do; and that was eat fruit from the forbidden tree. Adam would have to touch the tree to take care of it. Can you see how Eve added to what God said?

The second thing I want you to see is Satan blatantly lied. He said, "You will not surely die." I just want to scream from the rooftop, "LIAR, LIAR PANTS ON FIRE!" He LIED! Then he went on to tell another lie. He said, "For God knows that when you eat of the forbidden tree…. your eyes will be opened, and you will be like God knowing good and evil." You see, one lie always leads to another lie. Adam and Eve were **already** like God because they were made in His image. God created them for a world without sin, a world without sickness and death, and a world where nothing separated them from seeing God face to face. They knew nothing of evil. Satan deceived Eve with lies.

I want you to know he still uses the same bag of tricks on you and me. He twists God's Word around to make us doubt. He lies and tries to make us think God is holding out on us. I can assure you God will never hold back anything good from you. If it is good *for* you, He will make sure He gets it *to* you!

Satan's smooth-talking lies must have been hypnotizing. We see the results of his influence in Genesis *3:6-7.*

"When the woman saw that the fruit of the tree was good for food and pleasing to the eye, and also desirable for gaining wisdom, she took some and ate it. She also gave some to her husband, who was with her, and he ate it. Then the eyes of both of them were opened, and they realized they were naked; so, they sewed fig leaves together and made coverings for themselves." (NIV)

SIN AND ITS PROGRESSION

There is a progression to sin. If you can understand that now, it will save you a lot of heartache later.

1. The first step toward sin is doubting God's Word. Satan is always after the Word of God in us. He will do anything to discredit it. He tries to make us discontent with what we have and make us think God is withholding something from us. He knows if we truly believe God is good and that His Word is true, he has no power over us. He deceives and lies to lure us away from God. He never wants you to fulfill your purpose or your destiny. Do you know why? Because you will win people to Christ and make the world a beautiful place that looks like the Garden of Eden. If you want something you can be absolutely sure of in this life it is this: God's Word will stand when everything else passes away. (Matthew 24:25) You can depend on that!

2. The second step toward sin is compromise. Satan put thoughts in Eve's mind that God's Word could be added to or twisted. God's commands are nonnegotiable for a reason. God's laws are for our good and our protection. Satan knows if he can get us to let down our guard he can slither in and cause us to cave in. He plays tricks

on our minds and that is why it is so important to renew our minds daily so we will not play into his hands. (Romans 12:2) We need to know what the Bible teaches us for ourselves so we cannot be misled.

3. Doubting God's Word leads to compromise and compromise leads to falling into the trap of lust. Lust is a strong, powerful desire or craving. Eve **saw** that the fruit of the tree was good and pleasing to the eye. Lust begins with what we see. Many times, the devil will tempt you with something that will take your attention away from God. What is tempting to you may not tempt me at all. For example, if you put a bag of Oreos in front of me, I can walk past them without thinking of them at all. But if you put a pan of homemade chocolate chip cookies right out of the oven on the counter … now **that** is a different story! It would be very difficult for me to pass them up! I would immediately have a strong, powerful desire for warm chocolate chip cookies! Satan will not tempt you with something that you don't like. He makes it look really good. When you linger too long looking at anything that takes your attention and your affection away from God, it will become a snare and a trap. BEWARE! Have you ever been watching TV and a commercial comes on advertising a great big juicy hamburger? Then you start craving a hamburger for the next few days until you find yourself pulling up to that exact restaurant ordering the hamburger you saw on the commercial a couple nights ago! That is the power of visual influence. Cookies and hamburgers are innocent enough. But what about sexual influences? What about partying and drug influences? Be careful what you watch because it can have a magnetic pull in your imagination causing you to eventually act on what you see.

4. The fruit from the forbidden tree was pleasing to Eve's eye and she spent too much time around it until it was all she could think about, and it became something she could not deny. That led Eve

to act on what she looked upon. The next step toward sin was Eve's desire for wisdom. In other words, Eve thought she knew best what was good for her. She wanted to make herself happy based on what her flesh was craving. It is a lot like that for most people today. Instead of looking to God for wisdom and meeting their needs, they live by the loose motto: "If it feels good, do it" or "I deserve to be happy." I'm sure you know while sin is pleasurable for a moment .... its consequences can last a lifetime. Sin and consequences come as a package deal. The devil hides the consequences from you while he dangles the fun part in front of you. That is the power of sin. It looks good. It feels good. **Until it doesn't**. Sin never ends well. The Bible clearly warns us the end result of sin is death. (Romans 6:23)

5. Doubting God's Word leads to compromise which leads to lust which leads to ignoring God's boundaries and making decisions based on feelings and cravings which leads to acting out the sin. Eve fell into this progression of sin and Genesis 3:6 tells us the outcome...she took the forbidden fruit and ate it. She also gave some to her husband and he ate it. They both disobeyed God. Notice Eve did not eat the fruit by herself. She offered it to Adam, and he ate it too. Sin likes company and wants to take down as many people as it can.

6. The consequences. Lastly, we see the consequences of their disobedience. *Their eyes were opened, and they realized they were naked; so, they sewed fig leaves together and made coverings for themselves.* (Genesis 3:7) Once we cross the line of sin, guilt and shame are immediate companions. Adam and Eve had nothing to hide from God before they sinned. Being "naked" before God is standing before him unashamed. As soon as they ate the forbidden fruit the result of their sin was shame. That is why they tried to cover themselves with fig leaves. Who told them they were naked? Who told them they needed cover? God didn't. It was the voice of shame. Have you ever felt guilt or shame? It is a terrible feeling, isn't it? And the

devil loves it! Shame makes you want to run and hide. It makes you keep secrets. You try to cover it up with lies. Before you know it one lie leads to another, and it becomes exhausting living in all the mess you made. The devil tries everything he can to get you to cross the line of disobedience so you will live with shackles of guilt and shame. He knows it will be his best shot at keeping you away from God. Jesus tells us the devil is a thief who comes to kill, steal, and destroy. (John 10:10) But right after that Jesus said, "I have come in order that you might have life—life in all its fullness." The devil comes to kill your influence, your reputation, steal your identity in Christ, and destroy your witness. Thank God for sending Jesus to the rescue! He came to give us hope, a future and a full life. If you have crossed the line by disobeying God and you know all too well what shame feels like, I want to remind you that is exactly why Jesus came. He came to restore us to God when we have been deceived and swayed by the enemy. If you have made it this far in reading this book, I believe God is using it as His hand extended to save you, to help you and to hold you. He wants you to know He is not mad at you. He loves and adores you and wants you to stop trying to hide from him because of shame. He will take your shame and put it where it belongs. Devil … shame on **you**. That is exactly where it belongs.

Can we stop right here and pray together?

Dear God,

I ask you to forgive me for ever doubting you and for the times I compromised what I know is right. Forgive me for thinking I know what will make me happy or give me self-worth. Nothing in this world will ever satisfy me or give my life meaning. That can only come from you. Forgive me for all the times I have failed you and disobeyed you. Thank you for taking my guilt and shame and for giving me another chance to stand before you with a clean conscience. Thank you for loving me even when I have not acknowledged you. Help me to live my life in a way that it pleases you. Amen.

By now you understand how we were separated from God in the beginning and how Satan continues to go after God's people. Satan cannot touch God, so he tries to take down His kids. Jesus came to expose the devil and make a way for us back to God. His death on the cross paid the price for you and me to be free. That, my friend is what it means to be redeemed. All because you are CHOSEN.

Isaiah 43:1

Fear not: for I have redeemed you.

I have called you by name; you are mine.

God knew you before you were ever born. I know that is hard to fathom. But I find it comforting to know that God, who created the universe, is the same God who said, "Let there be light" and there was light and to this very day that light still exists; is the same God who divided the land and the oceans and gives the oceans their boundaries; is the same God who created all forms of animal life and plant life and sustains them through thousands of years; is the same God who flung the stars and galaxies into place and knows them by name… That same God … thought of you … and He proclaimed, "I don't have a (Put your name here.) I need her because I have this plan and I need her to execute it."

He said, "I know the plans I have for you…. plans to prosper you…. not to harm you…plans to give you hope and a future." (Jeremiah 29:11 NIV)

Isn't that the most incredible thought?

The same God who knows the stars and galaxies by name knows the number of hairs on your head! I find that quite comical and you would too if you saw my hairbrush!

Luke 12 gives an account of Jesus teaching a large crowd of people who gathered around him to draw from his wisdom. On this particular day he was teaching the people about fear. The main point of His message was we should not fear people, rather we should fear God. Of course, the phrase, "fear God" doesn't mean we should be afraid of God, rather it means respect God by acknowledging He is the One who determines your eternal destiny. But remember this: this loving God cares for you deeply.

It was right in the middle of this discussion Jesus made this point:

Luke 12:6 "What is the price of five sparrows- two copper coins? Yet God does not forget a single one of them. The very hairs on your head have all been numbered. Don't be afraid! You are worth more than many sparrows" (NLT)

You see, sparrows were sold for food. They were very common and very affordable. Five sparrows for two pennies-- that is a deal! Jesus was making the point that even the sparrows as common and inexpensive as they were, are all known by God. Each one of them matters to God. Then he compared the common little bird to the number of hairs on our heads. Jesus said every single strand of hair is counted by God. I find that amazing because we all lose strands of hair every day! But Jesus is making the point like the common sparrows, like the hairs on your head, you are known, and you count to God. You matter. You are seen. You are valued.

Jesus was trying to convey this major idea: who you fear (respect) determines how you live and what you do. You should never fear people more than you fear God. In other words, don't give people more power over you and your decisions than you give God. People don't know you like God knows you. He knows everything about you and yet He still loves you and wants the best for you.

The 3 key points that I hope you will remember from this verse are:

1. Don't fear people who have no power over you. Don't fear what they think about you. Only God determines your worth. People cannot stop God's plans for you.

2. Fear God (respect Him) for He determines your eternal destiny. We don't shrink back in fear when we approach God; but we DO lean into Him and surrender to His will for us. God's Word and prayer will serve as our compass in life keeping us on the right path.

3. Be certain of this: **HE KNOWS YOU.** He cares for you. He is your loving Father. He carefully watches over you to guide you day after day. God is good at being God. Therefore, there is no reason for you to fear.

Beautiful Girl…. You are seen by God.

Every hair on your head is counted. If God pays that much attention to every strand of hair, how much more does He carefully watch over all the other things that concern you?

You are so very loved.

YOU ARE CHOSEN.

YOU ARE CALLED.

DIVING IN DEEPER

Have you ever felt "unseen?" What were the circumstances?

How does it make you feel to know God knew you and chose you before you were even born?

If God knows exactly how many hairs are on your head, don't you think He knows everything else about you and what you are going through right now? If God provides for little common sparrow birds which are only worth two pennies …. how much more do you think you matter to Him? Take time to write out anything that is weighing heavy on your heart and give it to God. Is there anything you fear or dread about the future? Tell Him about it here.

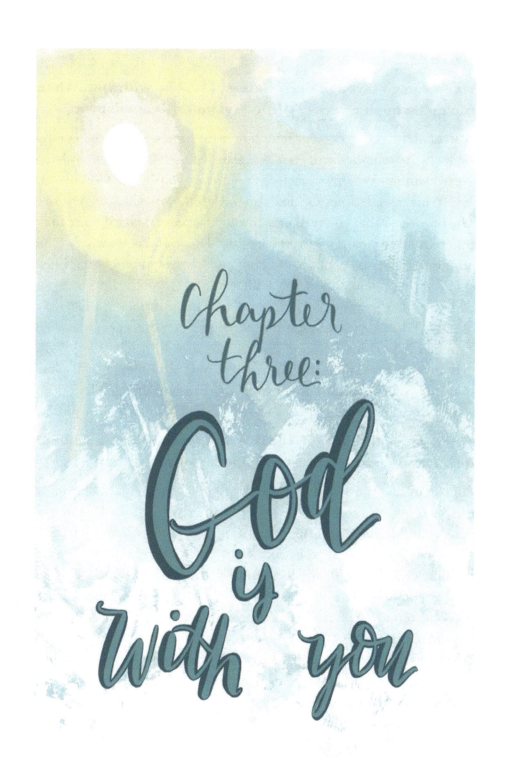

Isaiah 43:2

When you go through deep waters, I will be with you. When you go through rivers of difficulty, you will not drown.

Waters and rivers represent temptations of Satan. When the enemy comes with temptation it can feel like a flood because it feels so overwhelming. When you feel you're in over your head, God is with you. When rough times feel like rough waters, you will not go down. The promise is that you **will** pass through! Trials and hard times may come but they cannot overtake you. Do you know why? God promises, "I will be with you." Being a Christian does not guarantee a life without temptation or a life without trouble. But being a Christian *does* guarantee God's presence no matter what life may bring! We do not go through this life alone…God is always nearby. Troubles may come but God promises to turn it for our good. God does not cause bad things to happen to us but sometimes He will allow trials to teach us and become stronger because of them. When deep waters come, hold tight to God's hand.

When you walk through the fire of oppression, you will not be burned up; the flames will not consume you.

One of my favorite examples of God's presence in the midst of trouble can be found in the book of Daniel chapter three. It is the story of Shadrach, Meshach and Abednego. They were three young Hebrew men who were taken captive from their Jewish homeland and carried to Babylon. They worshipped God. Nebuchadnezzar, the king of Babylon did not. He worshiped false gods which were manmade gods that had no power. One day King Neb made a tall statue of himself out of gold. It was as tall as a nine-story building! The statue stood in the middle of Babylon where everyone could see it. King Neb called for all the governors, judges, city advisors and other important officials in Babylon to come to the dedication of the statue he set up. Then one of the king's messengers made an important announcement: "When you hear the sound of music, you must fall down and worship this gold statue. Anyone who does not obey this rule will be thrown into a fiery furnace!"

This rule was for everyone in Babylon. So as soon as the people heard the music, all people of all nations everywhere fell down and worshiped the gold statue like the king commanded. Everyone except Shadrach, Meshach, and Abednego. They refused to bow down to a statue.

Some men went to King Neb to complain about Shadrach, Meshach, and Abednego. They did not like the three Hebrew boys who refused to obey the king. The news about the boys who would not bow made the king furious. He called for the three Hebrew friends. When they arrived the king asked them, "Is it true you do not serve my gods or worship the image of gold I have set up? If you refuse to bow each time you hear the music, I will throw you in a fiery furnace! Then what god will be able to rescue you from my power?"

The three Hebrew friends answered, "If it is to be, the God we serve is able to deliver us from the fiery furnace, and he will save us from your hand. But even if you change your mind and don't throw us in the furnace, we still will not bow and serve your golden statue."

This made King Neb burn with rage. The fire in the furnace was already very hot but he ordered the heat to be turned up seven times hotter! He called for the strongest soldiers in his army to come and tie up Shadrach, Meshach, and Abednego and throw them into the blazing furnace. The fire was so hot the king's soldiers fell over dead when they threw the three Hebrew friends in. Shadrach, Meshach, and Abednego were all tied up when they were thrown into the fire.

When King Neb saw his strong soldiers fall over dead, he immediately jumped to his feet. He asked his advisors, "Weren't there three men bound and thrown into the fire?" "Yes, King," they answered. King Neb quickly went to the door of the furnace. "Look!" he shouted. "I see **four** men walking around in the fire. They are not tied, and they are completely unharmed! The fourth man looks like an angel!"

King Neb went to the opening of the furnace and shouted, "Shadrach, Meshach, and Abednego—servants of the Most High God! Come out! Come to me!" So, Shadrach, Meshach, and Abednego came out of the fire. The king and all his royal officials gathered around them in amazement. They had not been hurt by the fire at all! Their bodies were not burned, and their clothes were not scorched! They did not even smell like smoke!

King Neb began praising the God of Shadrach, Meshach, and Abednego. He realized God sent an angel to protect and rescue his servants. They trusted God and were willing to die for God rather than bowing down to any other gods. And God saved them!

This turned everything around. King Neb made a new law for all people. "Anyone who says anything against Shadrach, Meshach, and Abednego's God will be punished. No other god can save people like this!" Then the King promoted Shadrach, Meshach, and Abednego by giving them high positions in the kingdom of Babylon.

I wanted to remind you of this story because I believe it will help you when you face times that challenge your faith in God. Isaiah 43:2 promises, "When you walk through the fire, you will not be burned, and the flames will not consume you." It takes courage to stand up for God and for your faith especially when the heat gets turned up on your circumstances. The only people in all of Babylon who would not bow to the golden statue were three young men. Everyone else caved under pressure and fear. How did Shadrach, Meshach, and Abednego do it? Where do you think they found the courage and the boldness to stand up for what they believed in even if it meant they would die for it? I believe they knew God personally. They had a relationship with God. They saw God work in their lives long before King Neb made a golden statue. They could testify about their God because they had a track record with Him. What about you? Can you look back in your life and see God's hand working and taking care of you? Are there times He has saved you from an accident? Has He saved you from a bad relationship or a bad decision? Are there problems you have seen Him work out for your good? You have made it this far in life. You would have not been able to get to this point without God's loving hand of protection. You are still here and that means there is still purpose for you. God loves you. His plan for you is greater than any problem you may be facing. Will you trust Him today no matter how hot the fires of adversity may be?

The three Hebrew friends were tied up when they were thrown in the fire. The enemy will try to do that to you too. He ties us up in all kinds of ways. Wrong friends. Wrong relationships with guys. He wants us to let down our guard and cave into temptation, so we get tied up in guilt. Then he turns up the heat of the fiery trial seven times hotter! Remember, sin is always progressive. You never get away with sinning just a little bit. It will always lead to more. But sweet girl, don't forget this one thing: there was a fourth man in that fire! God always shows up to help untie us. No matter what has you tied up and burning with guilt I want you to know Jesus is with you! He is a friend that will be in the hot spots with you. He will never leave you *especially* in times of trouble because you are standing up for your faith!

Remember this fact about Shadrach, Meshach, and Abednego's story: the only thing that burned in the fire was the ropes that were used to tie them up! They came out of the fire not even smelling like smoke! When you put your trust in God and refuse to bow down to anything else you will come out of the fiery trial the very same way! Nothing will be able to harm you. God is always with you. He will bring you out safely. That is the power of our God!

Last but not least remember this: the end result of the three Hebrew boys' stand for God caused King Neb to worship God too. The King made a new law requiring all the people of Babylon to worship the God of Shadrach, Meshach, and Abednego. I wonder what could happen in your school, in your family, and in your community if you decide to be as bold as these three Hebrew friends. What a powerful witness you can be by not bowing down to popularity! I want to encourage you to take a bold stand for God even if it causes you to feel persecuted. God will be with you and cause you to come out of it on top. Just like Shadrach, Meshach, and Abednego, God will promote you at just the right time.

Maybe the thing for you to do now is find two friends who are as committed to God as you are. You will find it much easier to stand for God when you have a couple friends standing on each side of you.

The very last statement in our Scripture passage from Isaiah 43:3 is this:

For I am the Lord your God. This is the reason why God would protect and deliver you. He declares He is not only God, but He is *your* God. He is a personal God. Therefore, He will defend and protect you. He will always be the fourth man in the fire with you. He will give you the courage you need to endure any trial or temptation and he will make a way of escape for you.

Fear not, for I have redeemed you-- Isaiah 43:1b

I have called you by name, you are mine. When you go through deep waters, I will be with you. When you walk through the fires of oppression, you will not burn up; the flames will not consume you. For I am the Lord, your God-- Isaiah 43:2-3a NLT

We covered a lot so far, haven't we? I wanted to take you to the book of Genesis to remind you God had a plan for you from the very beginning. He had you in mind before he created the world! God loves you. He chooses you. He calls you. I can't say that enough!

God's plan for you began with his plan for Adam and Eve. He created people in His image so they could fill the whole earth with His glory. God's glory is physical evidence of an invisible God. God's glory is the perfect harmony of all his attributes that demonstrate His goodness all wrapped up into one infinite and perfect being. Though we cannot see God with our physical eyes, we can see evidence of Him all around us and we can certainly feel Him. God wants to display His goodness to the world through me and through you. He wants our lives to be evidence that He exists, and He wants us to testify of His greatness. I like to think of Christians as living billboards advertising the goodness of God. Sometimes I ask myself, "Have I made God good today?" Have you?

God created people to love them and bless them so they could be a blessing. When we bless people by being kind to them, we will show them what God is like. That is exactly what God wanted from the very beginning. God wanted Adam and Eve to take dominion over the earth. That means He wanted them to rule over everything He created. I believe when God told them to take dominion over the earth, He was saying to take care of His creation; nurture it, love it, and enjoy it in the same way He would take care of them. In a sense He made them king and queen. His plan for them was for them to multiply. He wanted them to have a big family so they could love each other and work together covering the whole earth with people who love God and love each other. Of course, we all know that Satan slid in and interrupted God's plan by deceiving Adam and Eve and causing them to sin. But that did not change God's original plan for us. He *still* wants to bless those who love Him, and He *still* wants to work through us to bless everyone around us. 2 Chronicles 16:9 tells us, "The eyes of the Lord search the whole earth to strengthen those whose hearts are fully committed to him." While it is true God loves us and chooses us before we even know anything about Him…. He is searching for people who will also choose Him.

I was talking with my two teenage granddaughters recently (Lilly and Abby) and I asked them what they felt was the most challenging thing for their generation as a Christian. As they began to share different experiences with me, I felt a nudge from God to write this book with them because I realized they had a lot to say. I knew God was going to use their experiences and their voice to encourage others to choose God even when it gets hard. As we continued to talk about different things they face every day, I began to visualize them swimming against a strong current. The conversation with my granddaughters and the mental picture of them pushing against the current is how this book was born. Now you are holding it in your hands. I don't think it is by accident.

I read this quote by W.C. Fields recently and I thought it was very fitting.

"Remember, a dead fish can float downstream, but it takes a live one to swim upstream."

I want us to think of a rushing river as the symbol of life in this world. A big river has a strong flow moving in one direction. Let's imagine the day we are born we are placed in the water at the very beginning of this river. At that moment we are at the river's mercy. It feels as though we have no choice in the direction, we are going but it doesn't really matter because everyone else around us seems to be moving in the same direction. The problem is the river eventually ends. The destination is death and destruction. Here we are floating through life in a current we cannot control to an end we also cannot control. It's a lot like the dead fish in W.C. Fields' quote! But praise the Lord for the Good News of Jesus Christ! Jesus came to offer us a different life with a different outcome. Jesus came to rescue us out of doom and gloom and offer us His abundant life. The abundant life Jesus offers is life abounding in joy and strength for eternity. The day He calls your name He is offering you a choice: continue to float downstream with the world or turn your life around with Christ and start to *really* live! Choosing Christ does not take you out of the river. It just changes your direction and final destination. From that point on life will feel like you are swimming upstream against the current. Because as a Christian, you are! Following Christ and pursuing Him daily is a lot like swimming. We intentionally put our arms in and out of the water pushing against it and kick our feet to move ourselves forward. We must be intentional in our relationship with Christ to be able to continue swimming against the current. As we stay connected to Jesus, He will give us the strength to endure. It is important to be consistent on purpose because the minute we relax and stop swimming, we find ourselves heading downstream and caught back up in the current of the world.

For this reason, I want to help establish the main ideas in this section by answering a couple of questions. Exactly what is the current of this world and how can we stay strong in the midst of it?

~THE CURRENT OF THE WORLD

The world is more than just a round surface with land and water. The Bible speaks of the world in three ways; the planet (Genesis 1:1, 31; Acts 17:24), the people (John 3:16, 1 John 4:9-10), and the way the world operates. So, what is the current of this world that we are to swim against as Christians? The current is the system of the world; how it operates. It is a system controlled by Satan, where he opposes God and the work of Christ. It is the very opposite of everything of God. John, one of Jesus' disciples and the author of the Gospel of John, records Jesus calling Satan, "the ruler of this world." (John 12:31, 14:30, 16:11) The apostle Paul called Satan "the god of this age" in 2 Corinthians 4:4.

Remember, when God created the world, he made it beautiful with everything Adam and Eve would need for life. God wanted a continual relationship with them as he walked and talked with them every day. God gave Adam and Eve the authority to rule over the earth. It all went terribly wrong the day Satan found Eve standing by the forbidden tree in the garden. Remember he made Eve question if she ate the forbidden fruit, it would make her wise like God? Satan always makes you think sin is going to be good for you. She looked at the fruit and used her human reasoning to see that it looked good. That is another big mistake. Never use your own reasoning when making decisions for yourself. Temptation always presents itself to appeal to our senses and never includes the consequences on a warning label. Many times, what we reason is good for us may be good in the moment but can turn bad on us quickly for the long haul. God's Word will guide us into what is good for us now *and* later. Psalm 119:105 gives us the best advice about this: "Your Word is a lamp to my feet and a light to my path." God will lead us and direct us into what is good. We were never meant to live this life without God. God wants to guide and provide for us so we can live a full life with blessing and purpose. He wants us to depend on His Word for direction and protection. Satan knows this well. He knows he is no match for God. So, he goes after God's creation. He is so jealous of our relationship with God and how He blesses us. Oh, how he hates it! When Satan tricked Eve to disobey God and eat the fruit from that tree it caused a horrific chain reaction. It caused a great separation between God and his creation because God is holy, and he cannot coexist with sin. Shame became Adam and Eve's constant companion. Satan stole Adam and Eve's birthright. He tricked them to eat the fruit and it cost them the rulership of the earth. That is how the earth and its system fell into the hands of that evil serpent. That is why Satan is called "the ruler of this world" and "the god of this age." Everything you can think opposite from God and His intentions for this world was a result of Adam and Eve's sin. The garden that once grew beautiful plants and trees for food now produces thorns, weeds, and choking vines. Peace became invaded by fear. The greatest and saddest effect was sickness and death.

Satan definitely threw the whole earth into a tailspin. He created a strong current in the river of life with the intent to pull everything he can away from God.

~GOD STILL HAD A PLAN

Don't think for a moment Satan outwitted God. Satan may have fooled Adam and Eve, but he cannot fool God.

Ephesians 1:4 tells us, "Even before he made the world, God loved us and chose us in Christ to be holy and without fault in his eyes."

Sweet girl….do you know what this means? God had a plan all along. Even **before** he made the world! Long before Adam and Eve sinned. I know it's hard to wrap your brain around this. It is for me too! We will have so many questions answered one day when we see Him face to face. But for now, can we just trust Him knowing He loves us, He chose us, and He had a plan all along to deal with that seductive Serpent? God knew the result of Adam and Eve's sin and He was not without a plan for us. Their sin would cause a domino effect for generations until Jesus comes to rescue us out of this crazy world.

Oh, the love of God! How far reaching that He saw thousands and thousands of years in time, and He saw you. Yes, He had a plan, and His plan is good.

God is not like us. He is perfect and holy, completely loving and completely just. He doesn't make careless decisions or careless mistakes. He tells us in Isaiah 55:8-9, "My thoughts are not your thoughts, neither are your ways my ways. As the heavens are higher than the earth, so are my ways higher than your ways and my thoughts than your thoughts."

God has always wanted relationship with us. But we are not perfect or holy. That is the problem.

We live on a farm. We have horses and donkeys. We also have a Standard Poodle named Fleck. He likes to run through the pasture and roll in the grass and mud. When he shows up at my back door covered in mud, there's no way I can let him in the house unless I want dirt everywhere. He has to stay outside until I can spray him off with the water hose and eventually give him a bath. Just like I cannot hug my muddy dog and not get dirty, our holy God cannot be in relationship with sin-stained people. We are sinners by nature; spiritually unclean and separated from God. But because of God's great love for us, He made a way to bring us back into His presence. He made a way for us to be clean. He gave us Jesus.

No matter the year you were born, there is one thing you have in common with every person who has ever lived since Adam and Eve: **we all sin**. Romans 5:12 explains this for us, "Sin entered the world through one man (Adam) and death through sin, and in this way, death came to all people, because all sinned." (NIV)

All have sinned. Did you catch that? We all inherited a sin nature through Adam. In the same way you were physically born with blue or brown eyes that you inherited from your family, you also spiritually inherited a sin nature. But we are not without hope! God had a wonderful plan all along. John 3:16 shows us God's heart for us, "For God so loved the world that he gave his one and only Son, that whosoever believes in him shall not perish but have everlasting life." (NIV) The price of sin is death, but God could not bear to live in heaven without you! So, He gave His very best gift to demonstrate His love for you. He gave His only Son, Jesus, to take the punishment for our sin. "God demonstrates his own love for us in this: While we were still sinners, Christ died for us." (Romans 5:8 NIV) God sent Jesus to die on a cross for me and for you long before we ever knew Him. This is **amazing** love! God loves us even if we choose not to love Him in return. That is difficult to comprehend, isn't it? I can't wrap my brain around that.

This reminds me of a song I learned in church when I was a little girl. You may know it.

Oh, how I love Jesus.

Oh, how I love Jesus.

Oh, how I love Jesus.

Because He first loved me.

Oh, how He loves you beautiful girl! His love for you never changes. You cannot be good enough for Him to love you more. You cannot be bad enough for Him to love you less. He loves you unconditionally. I know that is difficult to comprehend too. But it is true. We might be tempted to believe that we are good enough to win God's favor or that we can do enough good things to counterbalance the bad things we have done. But the Bible clearly tells us "There is no one righteous, not even one." (Romans 3:10 NIV) If you lived the best life, you could possibly live without committing the "big" sins, the Bible tells us we are still dirty with sin. Even our good works are not pure. They are like filthy dirty rags. (See Isaiah 64:6) Thank God for His gift of grace! Grace is the help God gives us because He knows it is the only thing that will save us. There is absolutely nothing we can do to earn it or deserve it. Grace has a name, and his name is Jesus.

"For if, by the trespass of the one man (Adam), death reigned through that one man, **how much more** will those who receive God's abundant provision of grace and of the gift of righteousness reign in life through the one man, Jesus Christ." Romans 5:17

Yes, we all sin. Yes, we all inherited a sin nature which results in death and spiritual separation from God. And yes, we inherited it when Adam and Eve sinned in the Garden. What a terrible mess we would be…But God. The power of sin is no match for the plan of God. God had a plan to save us from Adam and Eve's fall. God's plan was Jesus.

I absolutely love The Message version of Romans 5:17-19. This translation calls Jesus our rescuing gift. Let the words from this passage of Scripture encourage your heart.

"Yet the rescuing gift is not exactly parallel to the death-dealing sin. If one man's sin put crowds of people at the dead-end abyss of separation from God, just think what God's gift poured through one man, Jesus Christ, will do! There's no comparison between that death-dealing sin and this generous, life-giving gift. The verdict on that one sin was the death sentence; the verdict on the many sins that followed was his wonderful life sentence. If death got the upper hand through one man's wrongdoing, can you imagine the breathtaking recovery life makes, absolute life, in those who grasp with both hands this vividly extravagant life-gift, this grand setting-everything right, that the one-man Jesus Christ provides?

Here it is in a nutshell: Just as one person did it wrong and got us in all this trouble with sin and death, another person did it right and got us out of it. But more than just getting us out of trouble, he got us into life! One man said no to God and put many people in the wrong; one man said yes to God and put many in the right."

Jesus died in our place so we could have a relationship with God and be with Him forever. But it didn't end with His death on the cross. Yes, Jesus died, and he was buried, but after three days He rose from the dead and *still* lives! That is the power of the good news of Jesus Christ! **He is alive**! Jesus did this for us because of His great love and compassion even while we were living in ignorance and guilt, weak and morally corrupt. Through Jesus, God made a way to restore us back into His original plan. He wants to walk with you and talk with you daily just like He did with Adam and Eve before they fell into sin.

Jesus is God's gift to us, a gift of forgiveness and restoration. But it is our choice to receive it or not. Will you accept this gift of salvation? If you are nodding your head yes, the Bible tells us exactly how to do that.

Romans 10:9-10 says, "If you openly declare that Jesus is Lord and believe in your heart that God raised him from the dead, you will be saved. For it is by believing in your heart that you are made right with God, and it is by openly declaring your faith that you are saved." (NLT)

~RECEIVING THE GIFT

"If you openly declare that Jesus is Lord…."

What does it mean to say that Jesus Christ is Lord? For Jesus to be the Lord of your life means He is the ruler or director of your whole life. He cannot be the Lord of part of your life. He must be given control of your entire life. All of it.

Think of your life as a kingdom and your heart as the throne. Have you ever seen a two-seated throne? Never! The throne is a chair representing the power of the king who sits on it. The throne is meant for one king. My question is will it be you or Jesus?

If Jesus is the Lord of your life, that means you must get off the throne and allow him to take control. It means you must stop trying to be the boss of your life and give Jesus his rightful place. He gave his life on the cross for you. That is a very high price to save us from sin and our own reasoning. I know this may be a different way to look at life. I know it can be hard trusting a God you cannot see. But I know you can feel Him. While we cannot see His face, we can see his hand working in our lives. Think of the wind. You cannot see the wind, but you can feel it blow your hair and you can see it moving all around you. It is the same when you trust in Jesus. You may not physically see Him, but you can feel Him and see the evidence of him moving in your life. We can also see evidence of God in others whose hearts and lives have been radically changed by the love of God.

When we give the throne of our hearts over to Jesus allowing Him to take control, our job at that point is to simply obey Him one day at a time. God's job is everything else. That is how Jesus becomes Lord of your life. It is that simple. Why do we make it so complicated?

Jesus is a gentleman. He will never force himself on you. He patiently waits for you to invite Him into your heart.

Let's do that together right here and right now.

Heavenly Father,

I confess today Jesus is Lord of my life. Thank you for sending him to die for my sins and thank you for raising him from the dead so I can live without guilt and shame. Forgive me for every time I fail you. Thank you for this wonderful gift that allows me to know you and experience you for the rest of my life and through eternity. Lord Jesus, I ask for you to transform my life so I may make you famous everywhere I go. Let my life be the evidence someone may need to believe in you. Help me to make my life all about you and not about me. In Jesus' name, Amen.

The Bible assures us if we believe in our hearts and confess with our mouths that Jesus is Lord we are saved. He came to save us from our old sin nature and give us a new nature that is in line with His heart and His ways.

Luke 15:10, *"I tell you, there is rejoicing in the presence of angels of God over one sinner who repents."*

Woo Hoo! There's a party going on right now in heaven all because of YOU! You just made the most important decision of your whole life! Pardon me while I put on my party hat and throw confetti celebrating with you!

If you prayed this prayer with a sincere heart, I want you to do two things for me. Write today's date beside the word amen. It will serve to remind you the day you were saved if Satan ever tries to make you doubt it. Next, I would love to hear from you. Would you please send me an email to let me know? Teresa@teresapritchard.net

chapter six: Set Apart

The moment you invite Jesus into your heart and make Him the Lord of your life, you become **set apart.** You no longer belong to the world; you now belong to God's family. Being set apart means you are saved and separated from the world for a special purpose. Set apart does not mean you are taken out of the world but set aside as a very special tool to influence the world!

I have a very special ring that belonged to my father-in-law. It is a wide gold band with a cross in the center. My father-in-law passed away two years ago. He was a pastor his whole adult life. He officiated my wedding, he baptized my children, and he stood with my family at the bedside of my dying grandmother and my sister who died from cancer at thirty-seven years old. He was a wonderful father and grandfather, and we miss him every single day. I wear his gold cross ring every time I speak or teach. I set that ring apart from all of my other jewelry because it is so special to me. It reminds me of how he was faithful in his calling as a pastor and how much he loved his family. Just before my father-in-law passed away, I had the privilege of staying with him several days to help take care of him. I asked him to pray for me because I wanted to hear him pray over me one last time before he went to be with the Lord. He stretched out his feeble hand and laid it on my head and began to pray the most beautiful prayer. He prayed for my husband and I to accomplish twice as much in our ministry together as he had accomplished in his. That prayer reminds me that I am set apart for God to do amazing things. I will remember that moment and his prayer for as long as I live. I wear his ring when I am speaking to remind myself, I am called, chosen, and set apart for purpose. It is not a ring I wear every day. I set it apart for the occasions I am speaking, writing, or any other ministry work. My gold cross ring is not common. It is very special. Just like you.

God has set you apart to live a godly life so the world can see the goodness of God through you. You are not like anyone else. You are very special. You are set apart to do amazing things. But I must warn you: when you make the decision to live for God, you will feel like you are swimming against the current for the rest of your life. Therefore, you need to become a strong swimmer. Being a strong swimmer requires as much mental preparation as physical training.

The Bible tells us "Be not conformed to this world, but be transformed by the renewing of your mind…" Romans 12:2

When you say yes to God, you are turning away from the world to follow His voice. There are a lot of voices clamoring for your attention, so you will have to learn to recognize the still small voice of God. That is the first step in learning to swim against the current. Next, you must no longer compare yourself against the world; you must compare yourself against God's Word. This is big. The world will make you feel you are losing out if you don't follow everything that is trending. You know the pull because everybody is doing it and most of the time without question. As you read your Bible you will learn to recognize God's voice speaking to you giving you direction, correction, and encouragement. You will learn to follow God's precepts instead of blindly following the crowd around you. It will take boldness and courage to be set apart but remember it is a great privilege. God chose you for this and He has great purpose for you. My gold cross ring reminds me of my father-in-law and all the ways he blessed my life and made it richer. It reminds me of his love and dedication to his family, his congregation and to God. I wear my ring to remind me that God is also using me. It reminds me to follow God's voice and stay to his course for me. I realized I will never influence the world by trying to be like it.

You have been set apart as holy to the LORD your God, and he has chosen you from all the nations of the earth to be his own special treasure. Deuteronomy 14:2

I want you to understand the difference in an orphan and child of God mentality. It makes all the difference in how you think, how you react, and how you live.

The Heart Of An Orphan Vs. The Heart Of A Son
Allowing God To Transform Your Heart

When we decide to follow Christ, we become children of God. That is our new identity. However, it takes much longer for us to begin to live that way—we live as though we are orphans instead.

The Heart of an Orphan		The Heart of a Son
See God as Master	IMAGE OF GOD	See God as a loving Father
Independent/self-reliant	DEPENDENCY	Interdependent/Acknowledges need
Live by the love of law	THEOLOGY	Live by the law of love
Insecure/lack peace	SECURITY	Rest and peace
Strive for the praise, approval, and acceptance of man	NEED FOR APPROVAL	Totally accepted in God's love and justified by grace
A need for personal achievement as you seek to impress God and others, or no motivation to serve at all	MOTIVE FOR SERVICE	Service that is motivated by a deep gratitude for being unconditionally loved and accepted by God
Duty and earning God's favor or no motivation at all	MOTIVE BEHIND CHRISTIAN DISCIPLINES	Pleasure and delight
"Must" be holy to have God's favor, thus increasing a sense of shame and guilt	MOTIVE FOR PURITY	"Want to" be holy; do not want anything to hinder intimate relationship with God
Self-rejection from comparing yourself to others	SELF-IMAGE	Positive and affirmed because you know you have such value to God
Seek comfort in counterfeit affections: addictions, compulsions, escapism, busyness, hyper-religious activity	SOURCE OF COMFORT	Seek times of quietness and solitude to rest in the Father's presence and love
Competition, rivalry, jealousy toward others' success and position	PEER RELATIONSHIPS	Humility and unity as you value others and are able to rejoice in their blessings and successes
Accusation and exposure in order to make yourself look good by making others look bad	HANDLING OTHERS' FAULTS	Love covers as you seek to restore others in a spirit of love and gentleness
See authority as a source of pain; distrustful toward them and lack a heart attitude of submission	VIEW OF AUTHORITY	Respectful, honoring; you see them as ministers of God for good in your life
Difficulty receiving admonition; you must be right so you easily get your feelings hurt and close your spirit to discipline	VIEW OF ADMONITION	See the receiving of admonition as a blessing and need in your life so that your faults and weaknesses are exposed and put to death
Guarded and conditional; based upon others' performance as you seek to get your own needs met	EXPRESSION OF LOVE	Open, patient, and affectionate as you lay your life and agendas down in order to meet the needs of others
Conditional and distant	SENSE OF GOD'S PRESENCE	Close and intimate
Bondage	CONDITION	Liberty
Feel like a servant/slave	POSITION	Feel like a son/daughter
Spiritual ambition; the earnest desire for some spiritual achievement and distinction and the willingness to strive for it; a desire to be seen and counted among the mature	VISION	To daily experience the Father's unconditional love and acceptance and then be sent as a representative of His love to family and others
Fight for what you can get!	FUTURE	Sonship releases your inheritance!

123

"The Heart of an Orphan vs. the Heart of a Son," Chi Alpha Campus Ministries, accessed August 19, 2021.

https://chialpha.com/blog/living-out-of-the-wrong-identity/

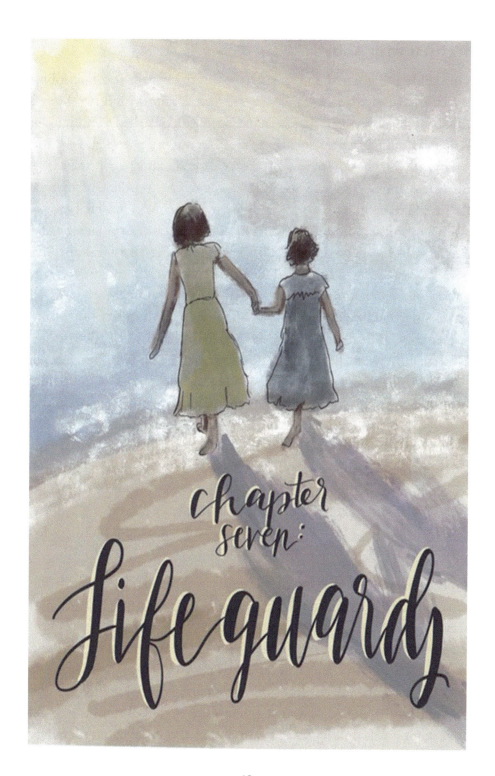

Written with Abby

One of the things I love the most about where I live in North Carolina is I can have my toes in the beach anytime I want within two hours, OR I can be enjoying the view of the Blue Ridge Parkway within four hours. My family and I spend most of our summer weekends at the beach. It's our happy place. My sister, Amelia and I especially love the ocean and boogie boarding on the waves. One year one of my best friends, Haden, and his family came to the beach with us. He has two younger brothers and the youngest is a modern day "Dennis the Menace." One day we were all boogie boarding and Graham (the youngest one) went a little too far out and got stuck in the rip current. (A rip current in the Webster's dictionary is "A relatively strong, narrow current flowing outward from the beach through the surf zone presenting a hazard to swimmers") Haden and I both tried to get Graham out, but the current was too strong for us. Our parents realized something was wrong, and so did the lifeguard on duty. The lifeguard suddenly appeared to pull him out of the water, and I couldn't believe how fast he acted. It seemed effortless for him. He was prepared to use what he had been trained to do as a lifeguard: to save people. His training prepared him to save Graham. No one forced him to be a lifeguard. He chose to save people every day. John 15:13 TPT says, "For the greatest love of all is a love that sacrifices all. And this great love is demonstrated when a person sacrifices his life for his friends."

God gives us lifeguards as we continue to live our lives against the current. Like the lifeguard who rescued Graham on the beach that day, we need to train so we can be prepared to rescue people from rip currents in their lives. We were all out in the water having fun and without warning there was a current under the water we could not see. Graham, the adventurous one was getting out a little too far and away from the rest of us and stepped into the pull of the rip tide. At that point it was pulling him farther and farther away from the safety of the shore. Can you see how this relates to our lives? We can be hanging out with our friends having a good time when one of them goes too far and gets stuck in a place that has way too much pull on them. Before you know it, they have gotten too far from the safety of the shore. They can't swim well enough to fight the current pulling them further away. Let me ask you, who are you swimming with? Think about the friends you hang out with the most. We need to make sure we recognize the spiritual strengths of our friends. Some are stronger in the Lord than others. It is important that we discipline ourselves to become strong in the Lord, so we are ready at a moment's notice to help pull the friend in danger out of a rip current and help bring them safely back to shore. Rip currents can look a lot like drinking, drugs, sex, eating disorders, and anything else that is lacking self-control. Rip currents can be deadly.

1 Corinthians 13: 4-6 says "Love is patient and kind; love does not envy or boast; it is not arrogant or rude. It does not insist on its own way; it is not irritable or resentful; it does not rejoice at wrongdoing but rejoices with the truth. Love bears all things, believes all things, hopes all things, endures all things." (ESV)

Love never fails.

When I think about this verse, I know that God is telling us exactly the kind of friend we need to be. It is saying, "Be like God." This verse is like the rubric on how to do that. The Bible tells us God is love. Therefore, God is patient and kind. God does not envy or boast. God is not arrogant or rude. God does not insist on His own way. (That explains why He gave us free will) God is not irritable or resentful. God does not rejoice at wrongdoing. God rejoices with the truth.

When we answer the call of God on our lives by saying yes to Him, He gives us a new heart with new desires. We begin to listen for His voice and follow the directives He gives us in His Word. We become more and more like Him every day. We will begin to reflect God in our lifestyle by the friends we choose the choices we make, our attitudes, and how we treat people. We begin to look just like our Heavenly Father. The Bible tells us we will be known as Christians by our love for people. (John 13:35) Sometimes I go back to 1 Corinthians 13 and insert my name as a test to see how I am doing. Try it. If you see something that isn't quite true ask God to help you become more like Him in that area. Think of this as lifeguard training.

_Abby_____ is patient and kind.

_____ does not envy or boast.

_____ is not arrogant or rude.

_____ does not insist on its own way.

_____ is not irritable or resentful.

_____ does not rejoice at wrongdoing but rejoices with the truth.

_____ bears all things, believes all things, hopes all things, and endures all things.

How did you do? Were the statements true about you? Now, don't beat yourself up. Remember, this is part of our training as lifeguards. We all need practice every day. As we know better, we will do better with God helping us.

1 Corinthians 13 is known as the love chapter of the Bible. It instructs us how to be a better person, friend, spouse, and parent. It is also great to use when you are dating or considering marriage. Insert your boyfriend's name in the blanks to see if the statements are true about him too. If most of them are not quite true, that would be a good

indicator his relationship with God is not what it needs to be and he most likely is not swimming in the same direction as you are.

When we have godly friends, they sometimes have a better view on our lives than we do. If you look too closely at something, it can be hard to make out what it is. Let me show you what I mean. Pick up this book and place it right in front of your face touching your nose. See if you can read it. There's no way you can see the letters and words clearly. It's all out of focus. But if I was with you right now, I could hold the book for you a little bit farther away until it comes into focus. When you have a godly friend as a lifeguard, they help pull us back from situations so we can see them better. They speak truth to us and save us from getting caught in the current. 1 Corinthians 13 is a great way to keep relationships in focus and we should remind our friends of this too. It is a great way to keep us from getting caught up in emotional dating rip tides. When Graham was okay and back on the sand, he admitted he realized how far out he was, but then it was too late. James 5:16 says "Therefore, confess your sins to one another and pray for one another, that you may be healed. The prayer of a righteous person has great power as it is working." In other words, pray for your friends even if they aren't in sin. And if you are struggling with sin, tell your friend about it. Confessing it brings accountability. True friends point you back to God if you are falling away. Ask yourself, are you guilty of not being a godly friend? I think we all are at times. I am thankful I have had godly friends who pulled me back and set me straight. Sometimes we don't recognize or appreciate the lifeguards God gives us.

~FAMILY

My meme is one of my main lifeguards. She shows me how great God is and opens my eyes to what He does for me. She's also really cool. She teaches me to never be ashamed of my faith; and to PURSUE IT. She has been my friend for my entire life. The Apostle Paul reminds us that even one parent or grandparent can have a great influence on you. Timothy was a young pastor of the biggest church in Ephesus. Ephesus was a large, booming city. Think New York City. Timothy was taught to honor God from his mother and grandmother. The apostle Paul-who was Timothy's spiritual leader- said this about him in 2 Timothy 1:5, "I call to remembrance the genuine faith that is in you, which dwelt first in your grandmother Lois and your mother Eunice, and I am persuaded is in you also." Timothy was blessed with 3 spiritual leaders in his life…. his mother, grandmother, and the apostle Paul. The foundation of his faith began at home and helped prepare him to pastor a large church at a very young age. This makes me think about my own family and how grateful I am to have a Godly heritage. I realize that not everyone has this loving environment. Godly parents are one of the greatest gifts from God. That's why in Exodus 20:12, God tells us to "honor our parents so that we may live long in the land the Lord your God is giving you." God literally tells us to honor them so we can have a full and long life in abundance. God gives us parents as lifeguards. They can see things from a better perspective and give boundaries to protect us. Have you ever been bowling with your friends or family and see a little kid bowling for his very first time in the lane next to you? They put up these bumpers in the gutter lanes to make it easier for kids just starting out. When the gutters are eliminated from the game, it gives everyone a chance to score. No more crying over a gutter ball! It gives you a better guarantee to score, but you have to accept the help. Your parents' boundaries are like bumpers…. they make sure you stay in the lane of God's will while you are still learning to hear God for yourself. They are God's gift to us because they love us and want the best for us, and they are willing to sacrifice their own lives to make sure we have a great life. That is why God tells us to honor them. Honor isn't a word you use every day. But since honoring my parents will guarantee me a long life, I want to know more about it! Honoring your parents means obey and respect them out of gratitude. If you have godly parents, you are blessed and there is no better way to show your thankfulness to God for them than to treat your parents as the valuable gift that they are. They are lifeguards to make sure you fulfill your destiny in God and live the full and long-life God intends for you.

~Honor Even if Not Honorable

I know, I know. You're probably thinking, "How do I honor my parents if they don't deserve it?" Honor is not obeying your parents no matter what. If your parents encourage you to do something illegal or something that could potentially hurt you, would that be honoring them? You can still honor them and not take their advice. Remember the definition of honor is showing respect out of gratitude. If you have no other reason to be grateful, you can be grateful your parents chose to give you life.

I found some very helpful points online about honoring your parents even when they may not deserve it.

1. Show them a healthy love. If you have a parent who lies or lets you down a lot, you can show them love by telling them how you feel and how that hurt you. You can also show them love by being kind. You don't have to fake "nice", but the Bible says to treat people how you wish to be treated, not how they have treated you.

2. Treat them with respect. Not only treat them with kindness but talk kindly about them too. Even if they don't treat you with respect, take the high road. They will make mistakes, but you should treat them the way Jesus would.

3. Forgive. Remember, they are human; not superhuman. Something my dad always says is "There isn't a book called, How to Parent for Dummies. We have to learn as we go." That always helps me give them a little grace. There's no excuse for abuse, mental or physical. If this is happening to you, you need to tell someone immediately, whether it be a school counselor or a

friend's parent. Anyone you trust. On another note, if your parents miss your ballgame or dance recital but have been to a dozen others, that would obviously be something to cut them some slack on. If your parents have been abusive, that might be harder to forgive. Just know that forgiving is more about you than them. They can say sorry and ask for forgiveness, but it is your choice to forgive. I know that can be hard and I admit sometimes I have to ask God to help me with it. Forgiveness is not letting another person who hurt you off the hook; it is freeing you. Remember that.

I want to encourage you if you do not have godly parents. God will provide. There are men and women God is raising up as spiritual mothers and fathers and He will provide what you need to continue your life journey. The Bible makes this promise, "You can be confident of this very thing, that He who has begun a good work in you will complete it until the day of Jesus Christ." Philippians 1:6 NKJV

Pray and ask God to bring a spiritual mother or father to you and begin to look for the answer to your prayer.

~FRIENDS

Friends are important because they have a lot of influence in our lives. We should be the friend for others we would like to have. God gives us godly friends as lifeguards.

My meme said there are three categories of friends: friends for a reason, a season, and a lifetime.

~Friends for a Reason

Friends for a reason will always be a gift from God. Friends that come into your life for a reason are sent to teach us or provide something we need at that point in life. Even if the lesson is what you should

NOT to do. Sometimes the lessons we learn from friendships that may not end well are painful. Choices may cause us to go different ways. I try to look at it from the perspective of what God is trying to teach me through the experience. I ask myself these questions: What did I learn about myself? What did I learn about being a better friend? What did I learn about God?

I always come to the conclusion that God can even use the bad situations to teach me and provide what I need for what is coming next in my life as long as I keep looking to Him.

I know for a fact that my cousin, Lilly was put in my life for a reason. She never leaves my side; she's a godly friend and my best friend. You may not even realize your friends were for a reason until the friend has left that chapter in your life. They don't always leave, but every once in a while, they do.

~Friends for a Season

Friends for a season come into our lives just like a season of the year. Think about it. Winter, spring, summer, and fall. Our lives go through seasons too. Winter is a time when the temperature is colder, trees are bare, and the days are short. The nights are so much longer in winter. We go through times like that in life too. Times when it feels like we are alone, and people seem distant. Times when things have come to an end. We need a friend during this time in our lives. And God will always make sure you have someone to help you through. They may only be in your life until that season ends but that was the purpose all along.

Think about spring. Springtime is new growth. Leaves are sprouting and flowers start blooming. It is a sign winter is over. We need friends to help us learn and grow too.

Think about summer. It's always pretty hot where we live. But it's a time for vacation. We need friends to help us learn how to relax and have fun.

And think about fall. It is a time when the leaves fall off trees. A time for letting go to make room for the cycle all over again. We relate to fall with starting back to school and advancing to another grade level. For example: we have to leave 6th grade to enter 7th grade. So, letting go isn't always a bad thing…. even though I will be the first to admit I do not like change. We need friends for this season too to help us in transition.

God will make sure we have friends for each season in our lives. And we need to make sure we become that kind of friend for someone else.

I don't like change. Not even a little bit. So, this topic is a little bit sensitive to me. It took me a long time to realize that change can bring good. A little over a year ago, my cousin, Lilly, moved about an hour and a half from where I live. Though it isn't very far, it was hard accepting she wouldn't be right down the road a mile away. Our moms are best friends not to mention they are also sisters in law. Lilly and I were born four months apart and we literally have been together our whole lives. We are more like sisters than cousins. Up until a year ago, we practically shared the same driveway. The farthest we ever lived from each other was four miles away. Four months and four miles. Now suddenly, my ride or die is over an hour and a half away. I spent weeks asking God "Why? Why did she have to leave?" Slowly, I started to realize that it was probably the best thing to happen to her and her family. Change will always be hard. That's how life is. But if you try to look for even a little bit of good, I promise you'll find it. Same thing with friends. When a season with a friend end, God isn't just going to leave you friend-less. It's just like the saying, "When one door closes, another one opens." Sometimes the season ends for that particular friend's influence in life. They might be good for you at the time, but once the purpose has been fulfilled, God will let you know that they were meant for a season. One more thing, if you don't have friend-screen (sunscreen) you could get friend poisoning. What I mean by that is this: sometimes you can have a needy friend that clings to you taking so much of your time that you lose touch with other friends and hobbies. They tend to isolate you trying to keep you all to themselves. This is never healthy. Most of the time you get burned. So don't worry about being friend-less or lonely. When your "season" ends, it will give you time to reflect on yourself and that friendship too! Some questions you can ask yourself are "Was I a godly friend?" or, "Was I guarding my friend's life, and taking them back to shore, or did I take them away further away from God? "Was I going to be in the rip-current of life with them?"

One of my favorite questions I ask myself is, "Did I bring this person closer to God?" If my answer is no, then I know to try harder with the next friends to come. One thing that I have noticed is season and reason usually tie together. When a season ends with one of your friends you can literally say, "God, show me the reason and help me learn from it." He may not show you immediately, but you will eventually know exactly why the season and the friend were in your life.

~Friends for a Lifetime

Lilly is in most of my part of the book, but honestly, it's because she correlates to the reason and lifetime categories we were talking about earlier. We may have arguments or fights, but it doesn't mean we are not still friends. That would just be silly if we disagreed and decided not to be friends. Is there anyone you know that will be in your life until the day you die? If so, you should make sure they know you love them. Friends for a lifetime are very rare. We take our best friends for granted and I think it's because of how truly close we get to them. These are the people who guard you the most. They are lifeguards that God has specifically assigned to you; and you to them. A lifeguard's sole purpose is to get you back on the shore. If the current is always pulling you toward the shore (the Lord), we wouldn't need lifeguards. One thing I hope you remember is LIFEGUARD=LIFETIME. Your lifetime friends hold such a position in your life and heart because they keep you in check to keep you safe. They literally stand guard over your life. They will let you know when you're not making smart decisions, but they will also let you know when you are by being your biggest cheerleader. Very few people have lifetime friends. That's why we can't take them for granted. We need to thank God for giving us people like Lilly. It's going to cost time and sacrifice to invest in having a lifetime friend as your "person", but it's so worth it. God is the common core that "knits" you together. A lifetime friend is rare because godly friends are rare. This all goes back to why we should strive to be a godly friend, because we need them in the world!

There's a duo in the Bible that exemplifies lifetime friends, and their names are Jonathon and David. They made a covenant with each other because they loved each other as their own soul. Being a godly lifetime friend is only possible when you love with a selfless love. It is a love that is sacrificial and gives it your all.

~David and Jonathon

The bible says that the soul of Jonathon was knitted to the soul of David. It was a soul tie. If you're reading this book and know nothing about David and Jonathon, you can find it in 1 Samuel chapter eighteen; but here is a summary.

Jonathon's father, Saul, was the very first king of Israel. He was the people's choice. By all appearances, he was a good choice. He was tall, handsome, and blessed by God. But Saul forgot that his kingship was from God. He made mistakes and decisions without consulting God, and it cost him the throne. God wanted to appoint a king who was loyal to Him. After God rejected Saul as king, He directed Samuel the prophet to anoint David even though Jonathon was next in line to the throne. I'm sure Jonathon was not the happiest about this, but one night David had dinner with Jonathon and his family and Jonathon practically fell in love with David's soul. I think Jonathon saw a reflection of himself in David. This recognition bound him to David. The world today would make this love and friendship impure. But he loved the God in David and he loved David selflessly. It was a love for his friend that was closer than a brother. I heard the expression friends are the family you get to choose. The love Jonathon felt for David was a love that caused him to empty everything out that was about him and yet he felt full because of David. We see the demonstration of this when he gave David his robe, his weapons, and his belt. These three gifts served as a sign of covenant. A covenant is a life-long promise and death is the only thing that breaks it. Jonathon's robe identified Jonathon as a prince. His robe identified him as royalty with all the privilege and power that came with it. When Jonathon gave David his robe, he was electing David as prince. He emptied himself by allowing David to have the robe that gave Jonathon his identity When Jonathon gave David his weapons, it represented a commitment to defend and protect him. Jonathon gave David his sword and his bow which was very significant in meaning. The sword represented strength, and by giving his sword, he was promising to give David his strength. The bow symbolized a person's power. Jonathon committed his and all of Israel's power to support David. The belt was the third gift Jonathon gave which was a very important part of a soldier's uniform. It was very functional in holding small swords, money and provisions, but the belt was also symbolic. The way it was woven together identified your status and accomplishments. Belts were given as rewards for bravery. Jonathon gave David his belt as a sign he had faith in David for many victories in the future. From that point on, the rest is history. They became best friends. David knew Jonathon was in essence giving himself to him and their friendship. The gifts Jonathon gave David served as a constant reminder of their covenant relationship and motivation to live up to the meaning behind the gifts. Jonathan never let jealousy get in the way of David and his reign because there wasn't any. There's never a place for jealousy between lifetime friends. You are happy for them, and you become their biggest fan. Your love trumps any jealousy you might have.

Love triumphs. Did you catch that? 1 Corinthians 13:8 says it like this: love never fails.

This brings us back full circle to 1 Corinthians 13. No wonder it is referred to as "the love chapter" of the Bible. As we receive the love of God, we must become what we receive. That is the only way we can love selflessly and pour ourselves out to make another person shine. I hope you will go back to this chapter often and test yourself to see if you are loving well. I know I will. We must not take our part of friendship lightly. The Bible tells us those who have friends must himself BE a friend. (Proverbs 18:24)

As we focus more on becoming the kind of friend we want, God will make sure we are surrounded by the godly friends we need.

I hope you recognize your friends and family as gifts from God. They are your lifeguards to watch over you as you continue to swim against the current.

Use this space to write a prayer of thanks for the lifeguards in your life.

~LIFEGUARD FLAGS

Godly friends and family are gifts from God. While they are not perfect, their love and care for us nurture our lives and give it significance. They are a reflection of God. In His loving care He gives them to us to help guard us, encourage us, and strengthen us.

But make no mistake, God Himself has His eye on you. He guards your life with His presence.

When I think of this river of life and myself swimming against the current, I visualize God's peace on one side of the riverbank and conviction on the other. God's peace and conviction are lifeguards waving flags and blowing whistles for our safety.

This reminds me of the time we went to the Great Wolf Lodge. It is an indoor water park and family resort. There are different water features for all ages. There are big water slides, wave pools, water coasters for the older kids and adults, and everything in between. I couldn't help but notice the lifeguards working the wave pool and the little kids play area. There were at least three or four on duty at each pool. They walked back and forth methodically with a whistle in their mouth nodding their head as they counted children swimming. They walked slowly and purposefully back and forth never taking their eyes off the children in the pool. I watched them for about an hour. I noticed the lifeguards would trade sides and continue walking back and forth watching the kids in the pool as they counted. As I continued to watch, I noticed a manager walking by with a life-sized baby doll that looked to be about two or three years old. He was trying to be discreet because he placed it in one of the pools as a drill for the lifeguards. Their response was being tested and timed. The baby doll floated the way a small child would if they were in trouble. The lifeguard attending that particular side of the pool immediately jumped in the water and rescued the baby doll. He went through all the lifeguard procedures as if it was a real child. Needless to say, I was very impressed.

God is watching over you just like that. He is attentive to your every move making sure you keep your head above water. He never takes His eye off of you. Psalm 46:1 assures us He is always present and ready to rescue in times of weakness or trouble.

WARNING FLAGS

I know we have been comparing life in the world to swimming in a river but let me switch gears for a moment to a beach scene to tie in warning flags. You've probably noticed the flags at a day at the beach. They are often located near lifeguard towers. The flags have different patterns of green, yellow, and red. Have you ever wondered what the beach warning flags mean?

Beach flags are pretty standard because they are mandated by the United States Lifesaving Association and the International Life Saving Federation.

Against the Current

God gives family to help us with safe boundaries and friends as swimming buddies, but God Himself is our ultimate lifeguard. He uses warning flags too.

God's peace

Colossians 3:15 says, **"Let the peace of God rule in your heart."** (NKJV)

That means peace calls the shots. Peace (or the lack of peace) decides what stays in your life and what goes. The Amplified Bible Classic Edition of this verse says it like this: "And let the peace from Christ rule (act as umpire continually) in your hearts (deciding and settling with finality all questions that arise in your minds, in that peaceful state)

When making decisions in life, God's peace is the green flag waving letting us know it is safe to proceed swimming. It may be a decision about college, a boyfriend, or a job. As you pray asking God for His direction, wait until the peace of God waves the flag to act. It will save you time, trouble, heartache, embarrassment, and so much more. And remember, the lack of peace is important to recognize as a flag as well. If you do not have peace about your decision, God is waving a double red flag! Danger! Danger! God is trying to prevent you from a life-threatening situation. One more thing to know: For everything God does, the devil offers a counterfeit. But make no mistake, he cannot imitate peace.

God's peace is a lifeguard.

Don't ever forget who you belong to: Christ Jesus.

He chose you. He called you. He redeemed you. He is with you.

He is your lifeguard for eternity.

chapter eight: Anchors

Written with Lilly

What do anchors do? I knew anchors stopped a boat from moving but I decided to look up the definition and this is what I found:

"When out to sea anchors help to keep ships stable in bad weather. They combat wind and currents that want to move the ship off course."

Like the weather, life can be unpredictable. When the storms of life come, I want to know I have an anchor that will hold me steady through the winds and rough waters.

Jesus said, **"Everything I've taught you is so that the peace which is in me will be in you and will give you great confidence as you rest in me. For in this unbelieving world, you will experience trouble and sorrows, but you must be courageous, for I have conquered the world!"** (John 16:33 TPT)

Jesus didn't hide the fact that as long as we are in this world, trouble is here. But He also assures us that He has won the victory over everything the world throws at us. Jesus said he "conquered" which is a very strong word meaning, "Overcome and take control of a place or people with military force." (Definition by Oxford Language) That would make the back half of this verse read like this:

"For in this unbelieving world you will experience trouble and sorrows, but you must be courageous, for I, the commander of heaven's army, have overcome and taken back control of the world."

Jesus came to take control and take back what Satan stole from Adam and Eve. He gave his very life in the battle against Satan, defeating sin and death once and for all. You may be wondering, if Jesus conquered Satan and the world system, why doesn't it look like it? That is a fair question. You can look around and see the effects of poverty, drug addiction, sex trafficking, confusion about identity, wars, and broken families. We groan for what creation groans for—redemption. Adam and Eve's sin cursed not only people but also the earth. In the same way sin was the beginning of the curse with all its effects, Jesus' death on the cross was the beginning of redemption. Yes, we were redeemed and yet we are being redeemed. Our full redemption will happen when Jesus comes back again. The earth and mankind are linked together. The earth fell under the curse because of the fall of Adam but it will rise because of Jesus. We also will rise to our full potential when Jesus comes again. He is coming and I believe it will be soon. We will be completely restored to God's original plan. And don't think we will be floating around aimlessly on clouds. No! We will be more alive than we've ever been! I believe we will continue learning, working, and worshipping. We will live without sin and death and most importantly we will live in relationship with God face to face just as it was in the beginning with Adam and Eve. Until then, we still live in a broken world with broken people. But we have hope...His name is Jesus. Jesus came to offer us a way out of the crazy current of this world. We have a choice: continue swimming with the current of the world or follow Jesus and get in the current of what He is doing. Two options. That helps explain the storms of life.

STORMS

Storms happen when a warm air front collides with a cold front. Thunderstorms are a result of moisture and differences in air pressure. This creates unstable air which can produce tornados. When we invite Jesus into our hearts, He begins to change us from the inside out. He warms our hearts with His love making us more and more like Him. He gives us new desires, and a new way of thinking. We learn to love and give. We learn to let Him have control of our lives as we obey His Word. We become part of God's family and we flow in the current of what He is doing in and through us. God influences the world through His people. He uses us to reach the cold-hearted world that is spinning out of control. He appoints us to help rescue a world that is being carried away by a strong current of sin. Two currents- two patterns happening at the same time. Good and evil. That is why the spiritual atmosphere of the world is so unstable.... just like colliding air masses. Until Jesus comes back, we live in a world where there will be storms. But don't let that discourage you or cause you to fear! Jesus is our refuge when the storms of life hit. We can run to Him and be safe.

What is your bad weather? Maybe it is social media, peer pressure, your friend group, anxiety, lack of motivation, popularity... the list goes on. Sometimes it goes from bad weather to storms that resemble a class five hurricane: like the death of someone close, parents separating, sickness, financial problems, or maybe the end of a friendship. Thank God for anchors to sustain you.

GOD'S WORD

My Bible is my biggest anchor because its message never changes. In a world where everything changes constantly, I need to know there is something absolute I can hold on to. The Word of God tells me who God is and reveals His character. God and His Word are inseparable.

John 1:1 tells us, *"In the beginning was the Word, and the Word was with God, and the Word was God."*

Proverbs 30:5 *"Every word of God proves true; he is a shield to those who take refuge in him."*

Matthew 24:35 says *"Heaven and earth shall pass away but my words shall not pass away."*

When storms of life come, God and His Word are anchors that will never fail us. No matter what storm you may be facing right this very minute, you can hold to God's Promises; and they will hold you.

We live two hours from the beach in the southeastern part of North Carolina. My family and I have seen a lot of tropical storms and hurricanes pass through. Our local meteorologists do a great job giving us ample warning so we can prepare for the storm in advance.

We make sure we have plenty of bottled water, groceries, and check our generator in case we lose power. We fill up an oil lamp just in case the lights go out at night, and we keep a couple flash lights handy as well. We usually have time to prepare for tropical storms or hurricanes a few days before we feel the effects of them. As they approach, we see the wind picking up and rain setting in. The winds and rain grow stronger as the eye of the storm gets closer and closer. I have seen the winds at eighty-five miles per hour before causing a lot of damage to homes and property all around us. Large trees would fall on houses, cars, and power lines. Many houses would lose half their roofs. There have been times our basement flooded with the water rising up to my knees. Even with all the warnings and preparation, it took weeks to clean up the damage the storm left behind.

I am thankful I know I can turn to God in times like that. Hurricanes can be scary, especially when they hit at night, and we lose electricity. We can't watch the news for updates or warnings. We just sit in the dark listening to the wind howling, rain pelting, and trees snapping as they are falling. That is when you will also hear me praying. Prayer in that moment is my anchor. I talk to God and tell Him I am afraid. I ask Him to watch over my house and my family. God is my anchor when everything around me is out of control.

This is the Promise I pray when I am afraid:

"When I am afraid, I will put my trust in you" Psalm 56:3 (NASB)

God's Word is a refuge when life hits like a hurricane. You can call out His name and He is there.

In the same way my family prepares our home for hurricanes, we need to prepare for storms of life. Reading the Bible and praying is the best way to prepare. You do it ahead of time by making it a lifestyle. When hard times come, and they will come to us all, we need to have an anchor set to keep our hearts and minds on God. The Word of God keeps us from being thrown off course.

Satan knows storms can make us question God. We may be tempted to think "God may be good but not good to me." Or we may ask, "Why would God allow this to happen?" We need to hide God's Word in our hearts so we can know and be confident of God's character. Just to be sure you know; God is always good. God is not a man that He would lie. Every promise He makes is true. You can depend on Him. It is so much easier to recover from a really bad storm when you believe God's Word which assures us that God is good and His plan for you is good. He will turn bad things that happen in life for good if we trust Him and stay the course. This takes resolve and that is difficult to find in the middle of the storm because resolve is a firm decision to stay on a course of action. It is much easier to get before a storm ever hits.

We have very hot, humid weather during the summers. Afternoon thunderstorms are pretty common. They bring a lot of wind, booming thunder, and sharp lightning. They pop up with very little warning and tornados can form quickly. It can be a little frightening because there's not much time to prepare for tornados. While hurricanes come with advanced warnings, they affect more of a widespread area lasting for days; tornados are dangerous because they are quick and so unpredictable. I have seen a tornado demolish a house on one side of a street and jump two streets over before it hits another.

I think of things like your parents divorcing or a family member dying with cancer like a hurricane. You can see it coming and though it is hard to deal with, you have time to process and prepare for it. It can feel like it goes on and on. You may never feel completely prepared to face it, but it didn't take you by surprise.

I think of things that happen that you never saw coming like tornados. Maybe someone you are close to was killed in a car accident. Or you find out your friend was lying and betrayed your trust. Maybe your dad was laid off from his job. Storms like this seem to come out of nowhere.

Predictable or not; the storms of life are scary and painful.

These are times we need a strong anchor to keep the storms from taking our faith off course.

I have been thinking about the anchors I turn to, and I want to share them with you to help you through your own storms.

PRAYER

I have to say prayer is the first anchor I hold to when storms come. My prayers during this time are not fancy or long. I just cry out, "God, help me!" Or "God, protect me!" Or "God, show me what to do!" I can assure you I have never faced a storm alone.

One of the Scriptures that gives me a lot of comfort during times of uncertainty or hardship is Psalm 46:1, ***"God is our refuge and strength, always ready to help in times of trouble."*** (TLB)

When devastating storms come, God is always a refuge. He is a shelter we can run to that isn't affected by our storms. He is our strength to help us stand the duration of the storm. He is always present and ready to help. That is why prayer is my first anchor. When you cry out His name, He is present even before you finish speaking because He is listening to your heart.

Psalm 145:18, ***"The Lord is near to all who call on Him...."***

~IDENTITY

There was a time in my life where I didn't want to get out of bed in the morning. I was so unmotivated. That was one of my biggest storms. I knew I needed to read my Bible and there were days I would look at my bible at night and say, "maybe tomorrow God." Little did I know then that my Bible was my anchor. The Word was going to support me physically and mentally through every storm but also keep me steady every day. But I was consumed with social media, trying to be at the top of the social pyramid. My papa says you are either coming out of a storm, you are in a storm, or there is a storm on the horizon. At this point I was in the middle of the storm trying to find my identity through acceptance and I turned to social media to try to find it. I wanted to be accepted by the community, but especially by the girls I thought were "cool". A lot of times I would read my Bible then once I felt comfortable with God I would fall back into old patterns. Waking up in the morning knowing this was not who I really was, was exhausting. I was so tired of putting on an act, but through it all I kept praying and asking God "Where are you? Give me a hunger for your Word. Get me out of this identity I know isn't mine." Prayer was the anchor for me through this season that I was so unstable. I never stopped praying. I didn't realize it, but God was working the entire time. The only thing I had to do was pick up my Bible and make an effort. I have come to realize if we make one small step toward God, He will be running full speed toward us. When I committed to reading and studying my Bible, I realized I didn't have to be consumed with social media. I didn't have to be popular, and I especially don't have to feel enough for society because I have been enough for God all along. I guess you could say I had an "Aha" moment. I realized you discover who you are by discovering *whose* you are. That is your real identity.

One of the days I was scrolling through social media, a sermon (by Lyle Phillips, the lead pastor at Legacy Nashville) caught my attention. I believe God wanted me to hear this message: "Only God has the ability to give you identity." He said, "If you give a human the power to give you identity, it makes it fragile." Wow! That message really made me think differently. I felt it was a message telling me to stop looking to people to make you feel better about you. Give your insecurities and weaknesses, burdens and storms to God. Let Him give you identity. That is exactly what I did.

Here's an anchor for you:

Psalm 55:22 ***"Cast your burden on the Lord, and he will sustain you; he will never permit the righteous to be moved."***

I learned once you throw all the weight of your "fake identity" on Him, He makes you feel enough, beautiful, worthy, confident, and his! Social media can make you feel like you are on an emotional roller coaster: up in the clouds one minute and free falling the next. It jerks your emotions all over the place leaving you whiplashed with insecurity.

The anchor of God's Word will brace you with truth; the truth of who you are and whose you are.

There are days where you feel like you don't know who you are anymore. Days like that usually happen when storms come and make us ask questions like: "Who am I?" "Why am I here?" "What does God want from me?"

Those are times we need to be reminded that our story is part of a bigger story. Before we can answer the "Who am I" question, we need to answer the "Whose am I" first.

WHOSE I AM

You belong to God. You are His.

When you know whose you are as God's child, you are secure in who you are because you belong and have identity. Satan wants you to forget who you are or at least confuse you about who you are but more than that he wants you to forget who God is. He knows the two are linked together. You cannot know who you are without knowing whose you are.

The times we question who we are, we need to remember this:

Job 33:4 ***"The Spirit of God has made me; and the breath of the Almighty gives me life."***

God is your **creator**. You would not exist if it were not for God.

Psalm 139:13 says, *"For you created my inmost being, you knit me together in my mother's womb."*

Everything about you was **God's idea**. God had you on His mind long before you were physically born.

1 John 3:1 *"See what great love the Father has lavished on us, that we should be called the children of God!"* And that is what we are!

2 Corinthians 6:18 *"I will be a Father to you, and you shall be My sons and daughters, says the Lord Almighty"*

You are a **child of God**! God created you because He wants you to become part of His family. Who calls us the children of God? The Father does.

Children of God are those who receive the love of Jesus and live a life of fellowship and trust with Him.

2 Corinthians 5:17 *"This means that anyone who belongs to Christ has become a new person. The old life is gone; a new life has begun!"*

The old life is gone; a new life has begun! That is great news, isn't it? We belong to a God who gives us second chances. Have you ever felt like you needed a do-over? Yeah, me too. When you live life trusting God and commit to a relationship with him, He wipes away the old life with all its failures. He gives us a new life with new opportunities.

This reminds me of bowling. When you roll the bowling ball down the lane and it hits the gutter instead of the pins, think about what happens next. The pins reset allowing you another chance. The reset happens after every attempt giving another opportunity to hit the pins.

Every day is a reset with God. The Bible assures us, *"The steadfast love of the Lord never ceases, His mercies never come to an*

end; they are new every morning...." Lamentations 3:22-23 ESV

Great is His faithfulness!

God gives us new mercies every single morning to do better than the day before. As we learn better, we do better. Our goal is to be more and more like our heavenly Father and to love people just like He does. This is what gives us our real identity.

WHO YOU ARE

Once I gave my storm to God, it was important to know who I was in Christ. I needed confidence.

Do you ever get that gut feeling in the pit of your stomach knowing something is wrong? That's the Holy Spirit. I know it sounds kind of crazy but there have been times when I was hanging out with friends, and they would say or do something that I knew was wrong. I was scared to say anything because I wanted to be accepted. Immediately after I do something or say something I know is wrong, I get the feeling of conviction. Conviction is the feeling of knowing something was wrong and it leads you to turn away from it and back to God. I recently learned there's a difference between conviction and condemnation. The first thing you need to know about the difference is conviction is from God and condemnation is from Satan.

Conviction is the inner voice of the Holy Spirit in our lives keeping us on the right path. His job is to help us not to stray. Conviction is a feeling that comes after we have sinned. It is a feeling of guilt, but it doesn't just stop there. It is a feeling of guilt that makes us want to change. That's important for you to remember because I don't want you to confuse guilt and condemnation with guilt and conviction.

Guilt in the hands of the Holy Spirit is a good thing because conviction is an anchor to keep you from straying. Guilt in the hands of the devil makes you feel shame and that shame brings condemnation. Condemnation is the feeling telling you to hide from God. It tells you he's going to punish you and be angry at you. Condemnation screams, "You are guilty!" It sentences you to punishment and judgment. The Bible tells us Satan is our accuser. (Revelation 12:10) He is the voice of condemnation. Condemnation is what he uses against us to put us in hopelessness and depression by making us think we have gone too far for God to love us or help us. It is one of his biggest weapons against us. The good news is we have an advocate in Jesus. He is our defense attorney when Satan declares us guilty, useless, and wasted.

1 John 2:1, ***"My little children, these things I write to you, so that you may not sin. And if anyone sins, we have an Advocate with the Father, Jesus Christ the righteous"***

The word Advocate here is also translated "Comforter" in reference to the Holy Spirit. So, think of Jesus as our Advocate (our defense attorney) with the Comforter (the Holy Spirit) standing by our side to comfort and defend us.

Condemnation leaves you standing before the Accuser all alone with no defense. It shackles you to guilt and shame which drives you further down a pit of sin. Satan will stop at nothing. He is ruthless. He wants you to self-destruct.

Beautiful Girl if Satan has handcuffed you with condemnation, let me reassure you of this,

"So now there is no condemnation for those who belong to Christ Jesus!" Romans 8:1 (NLT)

This promise is always a right **NOW** promise. I want to encourage you to memorize this Scripture. Whenever you hear the voice of Satan declaring you guilty, all you have to do is quote this verse. It will shut him up every time.

Where condemnation is the voice of the accuser; conviction is the voice of the Holy Spirit. Conviction is the voice of the Holy Spirit that corrects us long before we get in over our heads in sin. But are we listening? Condemnation screams "Guilty! Guilty!" Conviction lovingly whispers, "Turn around…stay on track…. keep your eyes on Me….and keep swimming!"

Condemnation shackles you to guilt. Conviction frees you from it.

Have you ever watched a cartoon or a movie where the character has a little angel on one side of their shoulder and a little devil on the other and they are both trying to tell you what to do? Most of the time in the movies you see the character deciding to do what the little devil says to do to get the plot going. Sometimes I find myself in that situation where I have a decision to make; to stand up for who I know I am in Christ and say "hey this is wrong guys…. and here's why" or the decision to go along with it and hide with that condemnation and guilt. I then have to remember there are storms of temptation and that I have an anchor, Godly discipline. Clearly, we know the choice we should make, but at the moment it's hard to side with the right decision when you feel like the only one making it.

Here's an anchor:

Psalm 27:1 (ESV) **"The Lord is my light and my salvation; whom shall I fear? The Lord is the stronghold of my life; of whom shall I be afraid?"**

God is always there showing us the right way to live. He is our light and our stronghold keeping us on course. Therefore, we never have to fear what other people think of us when we choose to go with our conviction instead of going with the crowd.

It is God's love that draws us to repentance. (Romans 2:4) He will not shame you. He rescues you. He does not blame you. He resets you. Remember, He chose you. He will never change His mind about that.

Know who you are because of whose you are!

DIVING IN DEEPER:

How does knowing the difference between condemnation and conviction help you?

WHAT GOD SAYS ABOUT YOU

Negative voices in the world seem to be louder than the voice of God. We need to be constantly reminded of who God says we are and our identity in Him.

Here are some of my favorite Bible verses that will remind you of your identity in Christ. I hope you will come back to these verses over and over when you feel overwhelmed or discouraged about who you are and let them speak truth into you.

CHILD OF GOD

John 1:12 "Yet to all who did receive him, to those who believed in his name, he gave the right to become children of God"

CHOSEN

John 15:16 "You did not choose me, but I chose you and appointed you so that you might go and bear fruit—fruit that will last—and so that whatever you ask in my name the Father will give you"

NO LONGER SLAVES

Romans 6:6 "For we know that our old self was crucified with him so that the body ruled by sin might be done away with, that we should no longer be slaves to sin"

GOD'S HANDIWORK

Ephesians 2:10 "For we are God's handiwork, created in Christ Jesus to do good works, which God prepared in advance for us to do"

FRIEND OF GOD

John 15:15 "I no longer call you servants, because a servant does not know his master's business. Instead, I have called you friends, for everything that I learned from my Father I have made known to you"

GOD'S TREASURE

1 Peter 2:9 TPT "But you are God's chosen treasure—priests who are kings, a spiritual nation set apart as God's devoted ones. He called you out of darkness to experience his marvelous light, and now he claims you as his very own. He did this so that you would broadcast his glorious wonders throughout the world."

YOU ARE BLESSED

Ephesians 1:3 "Praise be to the God and Father of our Lord Jesus Christ, who has blessed us in the heavenly realms with every spiritual blessing in Christ"

DEEPLY LOVED

Galatians 2:20 "I have been crucified with Christ and I no longer live, but Christ lives in me. The life I now live in the body, I live by faith in the Son of God, who loved me and gave himself for me"

YOU ARE UNDERSTOOD

Psalm 139:1 "You have searched me, Lord, and you know me. You know when I sit and when I rise; you perceive my thoughts from afar"

BEAUTIFUL

Song of Solomon 4:7 "You are altogether beautiful, my darling; there is no flaw in you"

STRONG

Philippians 4:13 "I can do all things through Christ who strengthens me"

SET APART

Jeremiah 1:5 "Before I formed you in the womb I knew you, and before you were born, I set you apart and appointed you a prophet to the nations"

GOD'S SPECIAL TREASURE

Deuteronomy 14:2 "You have been set apart as holy to the Lord your God, and he has chosen you from all the nations of the earth to be his own special treasure"

SET FREE

Ephesians 1:7 "We have been set free because of what Christ has done. Through his blood our sins have been forgiven. We have been set free because God's grace is so rich"

YOUR BODY IS A TEMPLE

1 Corinthians 6:19 "Do you not know that your body is a temple of the Holy Spirit within you, whom you have from God? You are not your own, you were bought at a price. Therefore, honor God with your bodies"

I pray these truths about who you are in Christ will be an anchor to hold you through every storm.

BACK TO THE WORD

Remember me talking about the Word of God being our strongest anchor? It is because we know it will never fail us.

No matter how many anchors you drop to keep you steady, it **always** comes back to the Word of God. Everything in life depends upon it.

Psalm 62:6 *"He only is my rock and my salvation, my stronghold; and I shall not be shaken."*

1 Peter 1:25 *"But the word of the Lord endures forever..."*

In a world that's full of constant change and unexpected storms these verses give me comfort. The Word of God gives me a firm foundation that will keep my life secure when everything else is like shifting sand.

~BUILD YOUR HOUSE ON THE ROCK

When it comes to dropping an anchor in a storm to hold me steady and keep me from going off course, I can't help but think of this passage of Scripture from the book of Matthew.

Matthew 7: 24-27 ESV

"Everyone then who hears these words of mine and does them will be like a wise man who built his house on the rock. And the rain fell, and the floods came, and the winds blew and beat on that house, but it did not fall, because it had been founded on the rock. And everyone who hears these words of mine and does not do them will be like a foolish man who built his house on the sand. And the rain fell, and the floods came, and the winds blew and beat against that house, and it fell, and great was the fall of it."

DIVING IN DEEPER:

I hope by now you can understand how important God's Word is to your life. It truly is an anchor that holds us.

Refer back to Matthew 7:24-27 above.

According to this Scripture, what makes a person wise?

What happened to his house when floods came?

What makes a person foolish?

What happened to his house when floods came?

The rain and floods came to *both* the wise and the foolish. I want you to see that storms come to us all. The outcome of the storm will depend on you.

What do you need to do to make sure you build your life upon the rock?

RENEW YOUR MIND

In order to build your life upon the rock of Jesus Christ, you need to renew your mind daily by staying in the Word and prayer.

Trust me sometimes it's hard for me to keep it constant and do it daily. Sometimes I struggle, but something that keeps disciplined in reading my Bible and prayer is remembering the benefits, and where I was before. My meme has always taught me the Bible has the answers to everything. I never really understood that until I really started reading my bible constantly. Have you guys ever experienced a hardship in your life and opened your bible and it relates to what you are going through? God has a way of getting exactly what we need to hear to us. I feel like God puts those experiences in our life to let us know he is a personal God. He sees us and he is working in our life. The Bible was my source of victory over temptation, my source for my faith, and my comfort. Those same promises are there for you too. Isaiah 28:10 teaches that God builds our lives "precept upon precept; line upon line; here a little and there a little." That means the Bible is our constant source teaching us life lessons of how to live one step at a time.

Romans 12:2 tells us, *"Do not conform to the pattern of this world but be transformed by the renewal of your mind. Then you will be able to test and approve what God's will is—his good, pleasing and perfect will."*

The pattern of this world belongs to Satan, and it has ever since Adam and Eve fell into temptation. Every person who is saved by believing in Jesus Christ, is saved out of that pattern and way of doing things.

Once we become saved, we have to learn a whole new way of living. We learn everything is exactly the opposite of what we once thought. Our renewed spirit now agrees with the ways of Heaven, but our flesh is renewed over time. In order for our flesh to come into agreement with our spirit, and the Holy Spirit within us, our minds must be renewed or transformed. That is the only way God's ways will begin to seem like the right way. Our minds must be renewed intentionally by the truth of God's Word. If your mind changes, you change.

Conformed versus Transformed

Do not be conformed to this world. That is a command. I want to make sure I understand what conforming is so I will not do it.

Conform means, fitting in, obeying, follow, to agree, to comply with rules, standards or laws.

Transform means, make a dramatic change in form, appearance, or character.

Now let's complete the sentence using our definitions.

Do not try to fit in to this world by following and obeying its rules, standards, or laws; but make a dramatic change in your character by renewing your mind.

Renewing our minds by the Word of God is the only way we can continue to swim against the current of this world. Some days feel harder to keep swimming against the opposition than others. Just remember there is a payoff. So, keep swimming.

And 1 Peter 1:13, *"Therefore, preparing your minds for action, and being sober minded, set your hope fully on the grace that will be brought to you at the revelation of Jesus Christ"*

This is another great Scripture about renewing your mind.

And a really good one.

We are told to **prepare our minds for action**. That means we need to be ready for anything that may try to make us stumble in our Christian walk. We are to gather up our thoughts, guard our thinking and keep our minds from wandering from the truth of God's Word. When difficulties come and storms of life hit, our hearts can be unsettled and cause our minds to be confused. The world's way of responding to storms is rejecting all that the Bible teaches us. It responds anger for anger. Rejection for rejection. You don't like me, fine! I don't like you. But for a Christian we have an anchor. We can be those whose mind is renewed daily in the Word of God, and we can remain calm and strong in the Lord. We become those who turns the other cheek, forgives an offense, and helps someone who falls into sin. A mind ready for action is a prepared mind saturated in the peace of God even in the face of trouble.

We are to be sober minded. What does that mean? I think of the opposite first. Maybe you've been around someone who was sloppy drunk. They stumble and fall all over the place. Their speech is slurred. They spill things. They are loud and unruly. Eventually they may even pass out in the middle of the floor. That is what our lives look like without God. Sloppy, undisciplined and possibly an embarrassment. But when we have a renewed mind, we are sober minded. That means we are urged to be self-disciplined; self-controlled; stable in our walk with God. That can only come from a heart that is trusting the Lord, eyes on Jesus, and anchored on Christ. We can live a stable life when we keep our minds on God and His principles.

We have one more step to follow according to this instruction in 1 Peter 1:13.

Set your hope fully on grace that will be brought to us at the revelation of Jesus Christ.

When you understand what hope is, you will see it as a powerful anchor! Hope is often misunderstood to be the same thing as a wish. Wishing for something to happen is having one foot on the side of "maybe it will" and the other foot on the side of "maybe it won't." Hope has both feet planted in agreeing with God's promise. Did you know the Biblical definition of hope is "confident expectation of good?" That changes everything doesn't it? By now you should know I am going to go back to the Scripture verse and rephrase it using the definition.

Help me do that here:

Set your hope (your _____ expectation of _____) **fully on grace to be brought to us at the revelation of Jesus Christ.** 1 Peter 1:13

Can you now understand how hope becomes a strong anchor? If you know you are confidently expecting good to come to you through a promise of God, you will not be wishy washy about it. You will live like it's a done deal and just a matter of time. That is how you can fully lean all the weight of who you are (and who are not just yet) into all that God is because you know God is giving you grace all the way until you see Jesus face to face.

We have the assurance Jesus will one day return for His church…and we are to anchor our hope (confident expectation of good) on this truth.

DIVING IN DEEPER

How does knowing that Jesus is coming soon connect you to the importance of renewing your mind?

Do you feel like you are "sober minded?" (Self-disciplined, self-controlled)

Are there any changes you feel you need to make right now?

Power of Prayer-Praying the Word.

One final anchor which connects it all together is praying the Word of God.

The Bible says God's word is alive and active. (Hebrews 4:12) When you use Scripture to form a prayer, it comes alive and works on your behalf.

I am going to make a confession. One of my biggest challenges is laziness.

Proverbs 13:4 talks about how the lazy person wants a lot but gets very little. This is very convicting to me. I want so much from God, and I want to please Him. But I cannot be lazy in my Christian walk. I realize I have to keep swimming against the current or I will be swept over by it.

James 4:17 says ***"If anyone, then knows the good they ought to do and doesn't do it, it is sin for them."***

Ecclesiastes 9:10 says ***"Whatever your hand finds to do, do it with all your might."***

These two Scriptures take away all my excuses for spiritual laziness.

I have learned I need to use Scripture as a basis for my prayers. Think of praying the Word as a two-winged bird. Prayer is one wing and God's Promise is the other. Prayer is a great thing. But what would happen if a bird only had one wing? Would he be able to fly? He would flap that little wing all he wants but all he would do is spin in circles never getting anywhere. But what if he had both wings? Prayer and the Word of God. Now he can flap both wings catching air to fly. It is the same with us. I get much better results when I pray the Word of God. Now I realize it may take time to find a Scripture that meets the need of what you are praying for but finding it will always come with a payoff. It's never been easier to find a promise from God's Word as an anchor. You can google to find Scriptures that speak about fear, hope, laziness, friendships; the list is endless. But I suggest if you google to find a list of promises, go to your Bible, and underline it. Sometimes I will put the date beside the Scripture in my Bible to help remind me when I was praying about that. When you do this, it will prove to you down the road how faithful God has been to you. We all tend to forget what we have asked God for. But He never forgets. When I use Scripture as my prayer, I know that is a prayer I can be sure God will answer. In His time. Recording it in your Bible is a great way to see God remembers His Promise to you and He is faithful to bring it to pass.

Jeremiah 1:12 gives me confidence God hears my prayers and is working to bring them to pass even when I can't feel it or see it.

Then the Lord said to me, *"You have seen well, for I am (actively) watching over My Word to fulfill it."*

When we use Scripture as a prayer, we can be sure that even before that prayer leaves our lips, He is watching over it to fulfill it. It will never leave His sight until it works on our behalf. We need to understand that it will come in God's timing for our good. If it is good for us, He will get it to us.

If you struggle with fear, temptation, insecurity or any other storm, the Word will always have the answers. Find your Promises in Scripture, pray them out loud and watch the fireworks of God in your life.

Father give me the motivation to do better for you and grow in your word. Give me a hunger for your word and remind me that whatever I do to do it with all my heart…. Amen

Psalm 18:30 *"This God—his way is perfect; the word of the Lord proves true……."*

Have you ever wondered what life would be like if you had been born in a different century?

Imagine if you were born during the 1700s to English settlers traveling to America for religious freedom. Think about how different your life would be. They didn't have electricity, phones, or running water. They didn't have indoor bathrooms! Life was hard work. Most people had to grow their own food and learn to be a good hunter to survive. The women and girls spent most of their time knitting and sewing. Men and boys hunted and fished for rabbit, squirrel, bear, and deer. Schools were one room classrooms with all grades lumped together in one room. Children worked hard because life was hard. They were needed around the homestead to help build and mend fences, plow the ground for crops, and skin animals. However once work was done, they managed to play games like, "London Bridge" or "tag."

God could have put you anywhere on His timeline, but He had purpose for you right here, right now.

While every generation has had to live through their own set of hard times, God's grace is present for the challenges they face.

Deuteronomy 33:25 says, "And as thy days, so shall thy strength be." This means God gives strength and support for the days we live in. Whatever the trials or difficulties may be, God is with you to bring you through. God will bring you through so you can help others through.

You are the David against Goliath, the Esther against Haman, and the Daniel against the lions.

DAVID AGAINST GOLIATH

You can find this story in 1 Samuel chapter seventeen.

The Israelites found themselves face to face with their enemy the Philistines. Goliath was a giant of a man from the Philistine ranks measuring over nine feet tall. Day after day Goliath stood and shouted before the Israelites, "Choose a man and have him come to face me. If he is able to fight and kill me, we will become your subjects; but if I overcome him and kill him, you will become our subjects and serve us. This day I defy the armies of Israel! Give me a man and let us fight each other!"

This happened every morning and every evening for forty days. Israel was being bullied by this giant.

Saul, the king of Israel, and all his men were terrified.

There was a man name Jesse who had eight sons. Three of his oldest sons had followed King Saul to war. His youngest son, David, was a shepherd keeping his father's sheep. One day Jesse called for David to take his brothers food while they were at the camp near the battle line. Jesse wanted David to check on his brothers and bring word back to him how they were doing.

Early one morning David left the flock of sheep in the care of another shepherd, loaded up food and supplies, and set out as his father had directed. He reached the camp as the army was going out to battle position. Israel and the Philistines were preparing for battle. David ran through the Israelite army searching for his brothers. Once he found them at the front of the battle lines, he asked them how they were doing. As he was talking to them, Goliath stepped out to the front of the Philistine army as usual shouting his belligerent threats. David heard it and noticed the Israelites were terrified and ran to hide from him.

David asked the men standing near him, "What reward is there for the man who kills this Philistine and removes this disgrace from us? Who is this man who defies the armies of the living God?"

They told him the man who kills the giant will earn great wealth and the hand of King Saul's daughter in marriage and he will never have to pay taxes in his lifetime.

King Saul found out David had been asking about the reward and Saul sent for him to stand before him. David said to Saul, "Let no one lose heart over this Philistine! I will go and fight him."

Saul said, "You are not able to go against this Philistine and fight him; you are only a young man, and he has been a warrior his whole life."

But David said to Saul, "I have been keeping my father's sheep. When a lion or bear came and carried off a sheep from the flock, I went after it, killed the lion and bear and rescued the sheep from its mouth. I killed both the lion and the bear, and this Philistine will be just like them because he has defied the armies of the living God. The Lord protected me from the lion and the bear, and he will protect me from the hand of this Philistine."

Saul said, "Go and may the Lord be with you."

David faced Goliath with his shepherd's staff in one hand, five small stones he picked up from a stream in his pouch, and a sling in his other hand.

Meanwhile Goliath with his huge shield in front of him, kept coming closer and closer toward David. He looked David over and saw he was just a young kid, healthy and handsome, and Goliath despised him.

Goliath began cursing David saying, "Come here and I will feed your flesh to the birds and wild animals!"

David said, "You come against me with your sword and spear, but I come against you in the name of the Lord Almighty, the God of Israel's army, whom you have defied. This day the Lord will deliver you into my hands. This very day I will strike you down and give the dead bodies of the Philistine army to the birds and wild animals, and the whole world will know there is a God in Israel. Everyone gathered here today will know it is not by sword or spear that the Lord saves; for the battle is the Lord's, and he will give you all into our hands."

As Goliath advanced to attack, David ran as fast as he could toward the battle line to meet him. Reaching into his pouch, he took out a stone, placed it in his sling and slung it striking Goliath on the forehead. The stone sank into his forehead, and he fell face down on the ground.

David triumphed over the Philistine with a sling and a stone; without a sword in his hand, he struck down the Philistine bully and killed him.

David stood over Goliath, taking Goliath's own sword, he cut off his head.

When the Philistines saw Goliath was dead, they turned and ran. Then the Israelite army pursued the Philistines killing many of them. When they returned from chasing the Philistines, they took everything valuable from the Philistine camp and kept it as their prize.

The moral of the story: When you know who you are because of whose you are, you can face any opposition that may threaten you and your generation. God will fight your battles for you when you go in the name of the Lord. God not only protected David in his battle with the Philistine but he used David to deliver the whole nation of Israel. Never underestimate what God can do through you! In the natural David was no match for Goliath. But when God is on your side, who can stand against you? David had an experiential relationship with God. When he faced the threats from Goliath, he recalled all the times God had brought him through dangerous situations in the past. That is where David found his courage and his faith to face Goliath. We must do the same. If you feel overwhelmed by a threatening situation, just remember all the times God has rescued you in the past. David's faith in his God gave him supernatural courage to stand before an impossible situation. God did not remove David from facing Goliath, but I believe it was God's hand directing that stone all the way to Goliath's head! Sometimes we must face our own giants. There are times we face situations that look way bigger than we are. We look like we are no match to win the battle we are facing. Those are the times we cannot look at what we do not possess within ourselves. We must look to how big our God is. Nothing is impossible with Him! God will direct you to your victory.

David's victory over Goliath became a victory for all of Israel. Your courage to stand up for God may be what helps many other people continue swimming against the current. They may see your faith and perseverance and become inspired to follow you.

You can be the David against Goliath for your generation.

DIVING DEEPER

What stands out to you about this story?

Is there anything in the story that you can apply to your life right now?

YOU ARE THE ESTHER AGAINST HAMAN

This is a story you can find in the book of Esther. It is a story of a young Jewish woman's bravery to stand in the gap for the rights of her people. Haman, one of the king's advisors, was an evil man who wanted to annihilate the Jews. The Jewish people needed someone to represent them favorably to the king. Esther was destined to be the one. She entered a type of modern-day beauty pageant in hopes of winning the beloved title, "Queen Esther." She was favored above all the other women and was given the honorable title and position of queen. Through a series of twisted events, she bravely approached the king on behalf of her Jewish people in an attempt to spare their lives. This was quite risky because no one was allowed to approach the king without being invited. She had not been summoned by the king for over a month. Esther knew she had to see the king and stop evil Haman's plot to kill the Jews. She fasted and prayed for three days while she mustered up the courage to see the king. God was with Esther and gave her favor in the king's sight. You will have to read the story for yourself to get all the juicy details. It is quite an interesting story with a lot of suspenseful twists and turns! However, in the end, Haman was killed by the gallows he designed to use to hang the Jews. I promise I haven't spoiled it for you. This is a must read you will have to see for yourself!

Esther was a young woman who decided to trust God. She allowed God to use her to stand in the gap for her people. Do you know what "stand in the gap" means? It means you go between God and what may be opposing Him. You get in the middle of it. Sometimes we have to stand in the gap for someone who does not know how to approach God for themselves. They may not be living a godly life right now, but we go to God on their behalf and pray for them. That is how you stand in the gap. You go to God for them until they do it for themselves. Like Esther went before the king on behalf of her people, we go before God asking him to preserve and protect our friends and loved ones from the evil plot of the enemy.

You are the Esther against the evil plot of Haman. (The devil)

DIVING DEEPER

Is God calling you to stand in the gap for someone?

Esther fasted and prayed before she approached the king. God honored her sacrifices by granting her favor in the king's sight. God will also honor you as you pray for those you are standing in the gap for.

Write out your prayer here:

YOU ARE THE DANIEL AGAINST THE LIONS

You can find this story in chapter six of the Book of Daniel.

The story of Daniel begins when he was just a young boy. However, by the time he was thrown into the lion's den, he was an old man. When Daniel was a little boy, the Babylonian army came to fight against Israel. Some of the people from Israel were carried off as slaves. Daniel and three of his friends (you would recognize the friends as Shadrach, Meshach, and Abednego) were captured and carried off to Babylon. They were very smart young men. The king of Babylon, Nebuchadnezzar, wanted them to work for him because they were so smart.

The four friends were dedicated to God, and they made it clear to the king they would put God first. They were put in prison even though they were very young, possibly as young as ten or twelve years old. They refused to eat the king's food. They knew God's laws and only ate food that God said was clean. They chose to obey God's law and refuse the rich food of the king. If they were living today, it would be like the king offering hamburgers, fries and milkshakes or steak, potatoes, and garlic bread with every favorite dessert you can think of! And imagine them choosing to eat salad or vegetables like broccoli and Brussel sprouts every day because they wanted to obey God's laws. To everyone's surprise, they were healthier and stronger than all the other prisoners who ate the king's food.

There were a lot of people during Daniel's lifetime who became very jealous of him. God's favor was upon Daniel and his friends and there were men who were jealous of their wisdom and power. Daniel and his friends were promoted to high positions in the government because they had a spirit of excellence. As time passed, a new king named Darius came into power. Daniel remained an important person in government even though there was a new king. The new king, Darius really like Daniel. He did not always agree with Daniel about his God, but Darius allowed Daniel to continue to worship God as he pleased.

One day Daniel's jealous enemies devised a plan to get rid of him. They could not think of a way to catch Daniel doing anything wrong because he never broke any laws. So, they decided the best thing to do was catch him with what he did right. They decided to make up a new law they knew he could not obey. But first they had to convince the king this was a good idea so he would sign the new decree. They went to King Darius and proposed a new law that said people could only pray to him or ask things from him for the next thirty days. If the king would sign the new law, these particular men committed to making sure the people would obey it. Of course, this appealed to King Darius' ego, and he thought it was a good idea. He loved the idea of the whole kingdom worshipping him. So, he signed the new law.

The punishment for breaking this new law would be punishment by being thrown into the lion's den. This was an underground cave where lions were trapped.

Daniel was a man of prayer. In spite of the new law, he bowed toward Jerusalem and prayed to God three times every day. The jealous men who convinced King Darius to pass the new law went to the king to complain against Daniel for not obeying. Though King Darius really liked Daniel, he knew the wicked men of his court would force his hand to punish Daniel. Seeing no other option, the King had to follow through and throw Daniel into the cave with the lions. The mouth of the cave was sealed with a big stone. King Darius was so worried about Daniel he couldn't sleep that night.

The next morning, he ran to the lion's den. He called Daniel's name and to his amazement, instead of hearing the roar of lions, he heard Daniel's voice. Daniel said, "God sent an angel to save me. The angel shut the mouths of the lions and the lions did not hurt me at all!" King Darius was relieved God spared Daniel's life. But then he burned with anger against the men who tricked him into a plan that could have killed Daniel. He commanded they be thrown into the lion's den and the lions devoured them.

Darius issued a new law that day that everyone in the kingdom should now pray to Daniel's God because his God was a savior, a rescuer and miracle worker.

Daniel was a man with integrity. He was willing to do the right thing even if he was the only person out of the entire kingdom doing it. Daniel would not turn his back on God. Jealous men plotted to get rid of Daniel because of his faith in God and his excellent spirit. You may never be thrown into a lion's den, but you may be thrown into a situation where people are jealous of you and are talking about you. The gossip against you may feel like the roar of hungry lions trying to devour you. I want to encourage you to be like Daniel. Keep swimming! Keep praying! Ask God to shut the mouths of the people speaking against you. In the same way God sent an angel to help Daniel in the lion's den, He will send help to you. God will turn the situation around for you if you will remain faithful. Remember what happened to the men who plotted against Daniel? Daniel was saved but they were devoured. God will protect your reputation and expose the evil against you if you will keep doing the right things. In the end Daniel was promoted and the king decreed for the whole kingdom to worship Daniel's God. As you can see, God not only delivered Daniel, but He delivered the entire kingdom from the lion's den. When you stand for God, He will use you as an example of His faithfulness so others will trust Him too.

DIVING DEEPER

Is there anything about Daniel's story that you can relate to?

Have you ever experienced someone being jealous of you? And have you felt jealous of someone else?

Daniel could not help that men were jealous of God's favor in his life. Even though it caused him to be thrown into the lion's den, he never stopped doing the right thing. God closed the mouths of the lions.

How can you relate this to your own set of circumstances? Does this encourage you?

You are the David against Goliath, the Esther against Haman, and the Daniel against the lions. Each one of these famous Biblical characters had flaws and insecurities. They were people just like me and you. They were not cartoon superpowers! They all had one thing in common: They held on to God! THEY KEPT SWIMMING.

There is a scene in the movie, Finding Nemo where Dory, a regal blue tang fish finds Nemo, a little lost clown fish, and brings him back to his overprotective father, Marlin. In the middle of celebrating the reunion, they notice a huge net sweeping toward them. It is a commercial fisherman's net. Before they know it, most of the community of fish are captured inside the net. Dory finds herself separated from Nemo and his dad as she too gets caught up in the net. Little Nemo has an idea to help rescue Dory. He breaks from his dad's grasp and swims between the holes of the net to join Dory and the others who have been captured. Nemo begins yelling above the scream of his frightened friends, "Swim Down! Swim Down!" He is trying to assemble all the fish to the bottom in hopes the weight will break the net to free them. Then Nemo begins to cry out, "Keep Swimming! Keep Swimming! Keep Swimming!" All the fish in the net begin to swim in the same direction toward the bottom of the net. It grew heavier and heavier under the weight of their concerted efforts until finally the net broke freeing Dorey and the rest of their friends.

Lilly, Abby, and I want to be the voice of Nemo in your life. We want you to hear us loud and clear…. Keep swimming! Keep swimming!

When all the fish inside the net began to move in the same direction, there was power for breakthrough. Breaking the net not only saved Dory, but it also saved them all. This is the power of unity.

1 Corinthians 12:27 tells us, "Now you are the body of Christ, and each one of you is a part of it." (NIV)

God gives each of us unique abilities and talents, but He intends for us to use them as a part of His body. In the same way we need all the parts of our bodies to function at optimum health, we need each other. I need the gifts in you, and you need mine. There are no lesser parts of the body; one part depends upon the other. You will think about this the next time you stump your toe! It's such a small part of the body but if you've ever hit your toe hard enough to break it, you know it gets your whole body's attention! You will do everything you can to nurse that throbbing toe and to protect it from being stepped on while it is healing. You may have to hobble along in the meantime…. but you keep walking.

We should have the same mindset toward one another as brothers and sisters in Christ. We need to respect one another and build each other up so we all can remain strong and faithful. When someone is hurting, even if it is pain, they created, we need to treat them like a broken toe. Do you know the best way to treat a broken toe? Usually, you treat it by taping it to a neighboring toe. This is called "buddy taping". This helps provide stability to the injured toe while it is healing. Nemo was directing all the fish in the net to move in the same direction. He was yelling for them to keep swimming to the bottom of the net. When Christians move in love toward a broken, hurting person and use the "buddy tape" technique, love helps to heal and break them free. Our friendship will help provide stability while they are healing. I wonder how many hurting people would grow closer to God if we would come alongside them and love them instead of criticizing or judging them. What could happen if we all started swimming down to help the downtrodden and surround them with love and encouragement? Like the movie scene with Nemo, I believe we would see the nets of sin, depression, and discouragement break. There is power in love and unity.

A lot of times we tend to look at ourselves and think we don't have what it takes to help someone. We may be tempted to think we're nobody special they would listen to. We look at what we are not instead of what we can be.

You may not be a great singer, painter, dancer, or athlete…. but there is one thing you can do that every person needs. You can be an encourager!

1 Thessalonians 5:11 (ESV)

Therefore encourage one another and build up one another, just as you also are doing.

We all experience times when we need an encourager—someone who motivates us when we want to give up, someone who stands with us when we go through challenging situations. Think of a time when someone came alongside you with encouragement. Do you remember how it made you feel? We need to focus on being an encourager for others. It is the most Christ-like quality we can have.

Here are a few ways you can be an encourager:

Smile.

Call for no reason just to say I love you.

Give a sincere compliment.

Share Scripture and pray for them.

Show them that you love them.

Remind them of their good qualities.

Be patient with them in their progress.

Don't' try to "fix" them: point them to Christ.

DIVING IN DEEPER

Can you think of other ways you can encourage someone?

Who do you know that may need your encouragement?

What is one way you could "buddy tape" yourself to them with encouragement this week?

Do it on purpose today. You may be the only reason someone keeps swimming!

LOCAL CHURCH

Another thing you can do as an encourager is find a local church that not only helps you grow in faith but also offers a place for you to use the unique gifts and talents God gave you. You need to find a community of believers that are also swimming in God's direction to help show you the way. I love the local church. I appreciate the different generations, races, talents, and levels of faith that are there. It creates a healthy environment for us to learn and grow. It gives us a place to belong. The local church is a beautiful picture of the body of Christ; each one working together to show the world what the Father looks like.

The local church is the place we find mentors to lead us by example as we do life together.

With one hand we hold the hand of a mentor to inspire us, teach us, and motivate us. With the other hand we need to reach for someone who may be one step behind us. This gives us accountability both ways. This makes us better swimmers and trains us for endurance.

Hebrews 10:36 tells us, "For you have need of endurance, so that when you have done the will of God you may receive what is promised." (ESV)

Acts 14:22 is very encouraging as well: "Strengthening the souls of the disciples, encouraging them to continue in the faith, and saying that through many tribulations we must enter the kingdom of God." (ESV)

Mentors are those who have been walking with Christ longer than you. They can help guide you and counsel you through many different decisions and circumstances. They are people who always point us to Christ and remind us to keep swimming. Many times, you will find a mentor in your pastor, a teacher, or someone who is like a spiritual mother or father. Look for someone who exemplifies Christ and consistency in their lives. Remember there are no perfect people but look for someone who deeply loves a perfect God. They will be a voice that can direct you to endure.

HOME

You will never regret swimming through every hard day. You will never regret staying the course. There is a reward with your name on it. We will stand before God one of these days whether Jesus comes back to gather his church, or we die in this earthly body. Nobody knows when that day will come but both of those things are sure things. We may not know when, but we know we will bow before Him. I want to hear Him say, "Well done my good and faithful servant" …. don't you?

Ecclesiastes 3:11 tells us God has set eternity in our hearts. That means God made us for eternity. We will live forever. There's a lot of things we can let go of and not be worried about if we are only going to live seventy or eighty years. But when you realize, you are going to live forever, it makes you realize what we do in this life really matters! This life is only a type of dress rehearsal for the real life to come.

The apostle Paul wrote most of the books of the New Testament. He was well acquainted with hardship, pain, and suffering. He was beaten and thrown in jail multiple times for preaching the gospel. He said, "For I consider that the sufferings of this present time are not worth comparing with the glory that is to be revealed to us." (Romans 8:18 ESV) He knew this life is very short compared to eternity and that he was only passing through to get to heaven where he would **really** live. Paul knew that while there is much to be enjoyed here and now, life in heaven with all the rewards God is saving for you would be far greater. He said you can't even compare. We need to always remember we are made for eternity.

James 1:12, *"Blessed is the man who remains steadfast under trial, for when he has stood the test he will receive the crown of life, which God has promised to those who love him" (ESV)*

Matthew 5:12, *"Rejoice and be glad, for your reward is great in heaven……"* (ESV)

Jesus is coming soon to take us to our heavenly home. There will be a mansion with your name on it and a crown custom made just for you. You may feel like you are swimming against the current here and now; but be sure of this; it will all be worth it, and it will lead you home.

One last thought before we end our time together here on these pages…. the only thing you can take with you into eternity is people. Share your story with as many people as you can. Tell them about Jesus and the day you invited him into your heart. Do your very best to make sure heaven is crowded! Make sure the people you love know you love them. Take every opportunity to tell them and show them. Encourage one another while we still have the chance to. When you can be anything… be kind…. and

KEEP SWIMMING Beautiful Girl.

KEEP SWIMMING.

About the Author

Teresa Pritchard is a bold, genuine lover of God with a passion to serve Christ and His people. Teresa is married to her high school sweetheart, Wesley, with two children and five grandchildren. The Pritchard's live on a farm nestled in the heart of North Carolina with their four horses, three donkeys, three cats, and a poodle named Fleck. They serve as lead pastors of Fayetteville Community Church which sits just a mile down the road. Whether you are walking in the front door of their farmhouse or the front door of their church, Teresa and Wesley make it feel like coming home.

Teresa has been teaching adult ministries for over twenty years and has written many Bible studies for women. She crafts breathtaking theme-based retreats for each Bible study she creates and hosts, with her most recent works being <u>Deborah: Becoming All You Can Bee</u> and <u>Against the Current</u>.

Teresa's loving heart leaves an impact on everyone she meets. Her greatest desire is for people to fall in love with God by falling in love with His Word. Like a true steel magnolia, she presents the Word with grace in one hand and practical steps of application in the other, making it personal to whatever season of life you may find yourself in.

For the past six years Teresa and Wesley have been restoring their farmhouse and barn, making it a place to share with the church and community to celebrate life's memorable moments. Perhaps their favorite spot on the property is around the black walnut farm table sharing meals, sharing laughter, and sharing stories. Just like the restoration story of the Pritchard farm, Teresa believes Christ has a beautiful, unique restoration story just for you.

Welcome home. Welcome to the table. Your place is set.